THE CALL TO RADICAL THEOLOGY

SUNY series in Theology and Continental Thought
Douglas L. Donkel, editor

The Call to Radical Theology

THOMAS J. J. ALTIZER

EDITED AND WITH AN INTRODUCTION
BY LISSA MCCULLOUGH
FOREWORD BY DAVID E. KLEMM

Published by State University of New York Press, Albany

For information, contact State University of New York Press, Albany, NY
www.sunypress.edu

Production by Diane Ganeles
Marketing by Anne M. Valentine

Library of Congress Cataloging-in-Publication Data

Altizer, Thomas J. J.
The call to radical theology / Thomas J. J. Altizer ; edited by Lissa McCullough ; foreword by David E. Klemm.
    p. cm. — (SUNY series in theology and Continental thought)
Includes bibliographical references (p.   ) and index.
ISBN 978-1-4384-4451-2 (hardcover : alk. paper)
ISBN 978-1-4384-4452-9 (paperback : alk. paper)
    1. Theology. 2. Death of God theology. 3. Philosophical theology.
I. McCullough, Lissa. II. Title.
BT28.A48 2012
230'.046—dc23
                                                    2012000730

10 9 8 7 6 5 4 3 2 1

We philosophers and "free spirits" feel, when we hear the news that "the old god is dead," as if a new dawn shone on us; our heart overflows with gratitude, amazement, premonitions, expectation. At long last the horizon appears free to us again, even if it should not be bright; at long last our ships may venture out again, venture out to face any danger; all the daring of the lover of knowledge is permitted again; the sea, *our* sea, lies open again; perhaps there has never yet been such an "open sea."

—Nietzsche, *The Gay Science* §343

CONTENTS

FOREWORD

DAVID E. KLEMM

Thomas J. J. Altizer is nothing if he is not a theologian. Indeed, he is the purest theologian of our time in his unrelenting concern with the name and being of God, and his theological thinking is among the most significant, original, and creative work of the late twentieth century and early twenty-first. In my view, Altizer is the successor to the great theologians of the Protestant biblical tradition represented by Karl Barth and Rudolf Bultmann, among others. In his own words, "the primary calling of the theologian is to name God, and to name that God who can actually be named by us" (*Living the Death of God*, 177). Such naming of God, for Altizer, requires unflinching honesty and courage, for the God who can actually be named by us in our time of advancing nihilism is only nameable as unnameable—a God who is absent, or nameable only as a negative presence, a presence so negative that we can speak of the "apocalypse of God" as the advent of absolute nothingness and darkness.

Who can deny that the great figures of modern literature, art, film, and other modes of expression confront and articulate the reality of spiritual desolation, of absolute nothingness interiorized in anxiety, despair, and visions of the abyss? From Kafka's *The Trial* and *The Castle* to Beckett's *Waiting for Godot* or the trilogy of *Malloy, Malone Dies*, and *The Unnamable*, to Arthur Miller's *Death of a Salesman* or Tennessee Williams's *A Streetcar Named Desire*, to the paintings of Mark Rothko

ix

or Anselm Kiefer, to Cormac McCarthy's *Blood Meridian* or *No Country for Old Men*, we see theological visions of the plight, pain, and violence of contemporary despair and meaninglessness.

Of course, many take refuge in simplistic ideas of God—say, the idea of God as a transcendent loving Father who looks after us if we pray and go to church. Fundamentalisms abound as well. Others take refuge in silence—having nothing to say about God. These ways of proclaiming or keeping silent about God, with all due respect to those who choose them, have nothing to do with the God who can actually be named and thought in our time. They constitute modes of withdrawal from the harsh truth, confronted, for example, by Elie Wiesel when he wrote in *Night* about watching the SS hang a boy he called the "sad-eyed angel" in the Buna concentration camp: "'Where is God?' someone behind me asked. . . . I heard a voice within me answer him: 'Where is He? Here He is—he is hanging here on this gallows...'" (76).

Altizer's task as a radical theologian is to comprehend the death of God as the actualization of the apocalyptic self-realization of Godhead itself. It should be clear to anyone who reads Altizer that he is heir to Hegel in trying to think the nihilism of the modern age theologically through the death of God as a colossal event in the life of God. But by no means can Altizer simply be called a Hegelian, as he transcends his great philosophical and theological mentor in crucial ways; for one, he appropriates the full power and ecstasy of Nietzsche's radicalized prophetic visions of nihilism in the late nineteenth century and beyond. While Hegel's *Phenomenology of Spirit* and *Science of Logic* fall short of disclosing the interior experience of the death of God in a world of advancing nihilism, Nietzsche does so not only in his proclamation of the death of God through the voice of the madman in *The Gay Science* (§125), but in thinking the death of God apocalyptically as, in Altizer's words, an absolute No-saying of God, an absolute judgment of God, as well as the transvaluation of all values under conditions of nihilism in the late modern world.

Nietzsche alone in the nineteenth century could think this absolute No-saying of God as at the same time wholly a Yes-saying, a Yes-saying to the absolute negation that Zarathustra proclaims. For Altizer, the *coincidentia oppositorum* between such an absolute Yes and absolute No, between the sacred and the profane, between ultimate light and ultimate darkness, is the central idea and image in his radical dialectical theology. Finally, such absolute Yes-saying to the absolute No of God's death in our time is, in Altizer's thinking, the actualization of resurrection beyond the death of God.

Editor's Acknowledgments

While a few of the essays published here were occasioned by a specific conference or project, most were spontaneously generated by the author independently of each other and with no particular publishing venue in mind. Nearly all were composed since 2001. In editing this book, my aim was to arrange them in an order that draws out their natural thematic coherence. The choice of book title is mine, approved by the author.

The essays are all previously unpublished, with two partial exceptions. Chapter 8 was published in French translation by Mireille Hébert under the title "Crucifixion et apocalypse" in the volume *Penser le Dieu vivant: Mélanges offerts à André Gounelle*, edited by Marc Boss and Raphaël Picon (Paris: Van Dieren, 2003), 9–17; the English version appears here for the first time, considerably revised, by kind permission of Van Dieren Éditeur. An earlier and shorter version of appendix B, "Altizer on Altizer," appeared in *Literature and Theology* 15, no. 2 (June 2001): 187–94; this segment of the essay is reprinted by kind permission of Oxford University Press. The present version has been updated by the author to address his publications since 2001.

I am grateful to several colleagues for their astute critical feedback and support of this project: these include Andrew Cutrofello, Alina N. Feld, Theodore W. Jennings, Robert S. Oventile, Daniel M. Price, and Carl A. Raschke.

—Lissa McCullough

INTRODUCTION

LISSA MCCULLOUGH

> This, too, is a unique calling of theology, a calling to voyage into our most absolutely negative depths, a voyage apart from which theology could only be truly vacuous. The theologian is a voyager . . . into the deepest darkness, a voyage apart from which every voyage into light is now wholly empty and unreal.
>
> —Altizer, "Doing Radical Theology" (5)

A living God inspires vigorous life and direction. A dead God bequeaths weight, disorientation, and appalling slowness—as when, enduring a nightmare, one feels unable to move. Already more than a century removed from Nietzsche's annunciation of the death of God as a remote event, a deed "still more distant than the most distant stars" (*The Gay Science* §125), we are understandably impatient. We "postmoderns"—surely a wishful self-naming—want to be finished with all this slowness and dead weight, as even a formerly liberating "modernity" has become a weight we pine to throw off. We long to advance! But we are stuck entertaining the very serious and respectable thesis that no forward movement to a truly new way of thinking and doing is possible unless we patiently, ever so patiently, revisit, reabsorb, reenvision, and slowly exorcize through a profound transformation the old—the centuries old, the millennia old—God. Any less patient approach to liberation from our past, generating and sustaining a new era, will be too superficial to succeed, no matter how intensely we hope and aspire to move on; too superficial, that is, to take hold and become effective, to give new direction that is not motivated by the old means and ends and styles of logic. This means contending with the gravitas of the past with a deep voyager's patience. According to this thought, we must abide with the slow decomposition and recomposition process until this abiding—a new thinking-believing-perceiving—gradually delivers us out of the valley of the shadow of death. It is not possible to force this deliverance through passion or brilliance alone. It will develop according to its own measures. We must be prepared to abide with what Thomas J. J. Altizer calls the "dead body of God" if we would be truly released from its infinite reach and power. The absolute cannot be overcome by being bypassed, evaded, or inconsequentially superseded, but only by being thought through and transformed.

This has been Altizer's consistent conviction through his fifty-year career as a death of God theologian. Hence he finds it exceedingly regrettable that theology has all but disappeared in our time except in forms that are predominantly conservative or reactionary—denying the death of God altogether—or focused on ethical rather than properly theological concerns, plying references to God and theology in ways that are vaguely assumed in support of an ethics rather than critically examined. "For the first time," Altizer observes, "we are bereft of fully systematic theologies that are critical theologies, and this is above all true of our fundamental thinking of God, which is now our most silent or most forbidden theological topic" (2).* As if echoing the ironic pathos of Slavoj Žižek's recent title, *In Defense of Lost Causes*, Altizer's cherished lost cause over the last half-century has been the reinvigoration of a genuinely radical theological thinking as against the overwhelming array of conservative options.[1]

If the question is, *why* retrieve theology as a mode of inquiry in the wake of the death of God? Altizer's answer is embodied in this book, in many passages explicitly and everywhere implicitly. The question of God is for Altizer the overwhelming question: the question that questions *us* absolutely. We need this question because it challenges us to activate our fullest critical and imaginative powers, conscious and unconscious. Apropos of this he acknowledges: "Yes, our most agonizing questions are what most impel a genuine theological language, and not only questions that are seemingly impossible, questions that truly assault their hearers with the most ultimate challenge, and if all such questions are dissolved in our common theology, is that not a dissolution of a real or actual humanity?" (139). For Altizer, it is in attempting to name a God who has become void and anonymous, in questing to create a theological language perhaps bereft of the name of God, in formulating such thinking freely as we venture forward instead of finding it preformulated, fossilized, and critically unexamined in our past, that we voyage toward an ultimate encounter and a truly new domain that dissolves the dichotomy between secular and religious, transcendence and immanence. He makes clear that a fully theological language pursued in this vein may be free to dispense with the name of God, and even with the word "theology" (135); it is the ultimacy of the call and the openness of the quest that is indispensable.

Altizer characterizes the present context of postmodernity as "a metamorphosis of the most purely negative forces in late modernity" (111). Mindful of postmodernity's critical contradictions and intricacies, he would concur with one commentator's insistence that theology must become "authentically modern" before it tries to be postmodern, otherwise postmodernity will be seized upon by "those who are reluctant to face the theological challenges of being modern" in order to evade the task.[2] Theo Hobson makes this culminating remark in his critique of the Radical Orthodoxy movement, but well before Radical Orthodoxy emerged in the mid-1990s, Altizer had articulated the same concern: "Conservative theologians can now laud the advent of a 'postmodernity' which is seemingly a dissolution of the modern world. But the simple truth is that a fully modern theology has not yet been written or conceived, so that there cannot yet be a postmodern theology, but only a renewed medieval, or patristic, or pagan theology."[3]

The writings of Altizer gathered here form a strikingly cohesive manifesto, one that poses a theological dare. The intent of this dare is to catalyze theology to reinvent itself as a mode of fully modern—and eventually postmodern—thinking; to radicalize it as a postontological, hermeneutical, imaginative discourse that is current and unrestrained, a creative thinking emboldened to rethink received traditions of the sacred, the profane, historical meaning, the human condition, the existential orientation of life vis-à-vis death, investigating how these actualities reveal an otherwise unhearable Yes and Amen: "Can such a Yes be pronounced today, and be pronounced so as to be heard? Is this not the mission of theology today, even if it can be realized only in the most radical theology?" (10). A radical theology is committed to think God, or rather the "God after God" of absolute transformation; not a primordial God of stasis and immutability, not a God of "Spirit" apart from incarnation, but a God who embodies the apocalyptic revolutions and evolutions of existence in time, who embodies actual history, suffering, change, death—ultimately Death—and therefore Life. In Altizer's terminology this God is named dialectically as at once Satan and Christ.[4]

Altizer makes the case that radical theology's keenest moment of historical opportunity is now. In the midst of this unprecedented epoch of apocalyptic transformation, it is possible for theology to stand *with* rather than against the forces of transformation—and even to lead them through visionary power. He offers a working definition of radical theology as a fundamental thinking that always entails the negative moment of unthinking on the way to rethinking:

> A genuinely radical theology is a theological thinking that truly rethinks the deepest ground of theology, a rethinking that is initially an unthinking of every established theological ground; only through such an unthinking can a clearing be established for theological thinking, and that is the very clearing that is the first goal of radical theology. Nor can this be accomplished by a simple dissolution of our given theological grounds, for those are the very grounds that must here be ultimately challenged, and challenged in terms of their most intrinsic claims. (1)

Altizer intends to demonstrate how the most exemplary models and resources for doing radical theology of this kind have been provided by continental philosophers—above all by Hegel, Nietzsche, and Heidegger—and by prophetic writers—above all by Blake and Joyce—rather than by modern theologians of whatever theological orientation, denomination, or school. Indeed, he argues, the most powerful philosophers and writers of modernity have been reinventing what theology is and can be in the modern world while theologians have tended to remain conservative and averse to contending with the full consequences of the death of God. In a post-Nietzschean world, those prominent theologians who have been regarded as most radical, such as the early Karl Barth and the early Paul Tillich, retained conservative positions in their maturity vis-à-vis the identity of God.[5] The modern philosophers and writers explored here, meanwhile, embarked on more radical and transformative modes of theological thinking, a quest of thinking not only after the death of God but precisely *through* the death of God (chaps. 1 and 9). For each of these major figures, the death of God is itself the core productive event of their epoch (see especially chaps. 3, 4, 5, 6, and 11). This cannot be said quite so fully of Barth or Tillich or any prominent theologians since, apart from Altizer and certain of his contemporaries influenced by similar cultural-historical forces.[6] In recent years the continental philosophers Gianni Vattimo and Slavoj Žižek have generated theological positions—still in rather fragmentary form—remarkably similar to the one Altizer has been elaborating systematically since the mid-1960s. Signs of their mutual influence and exchange are only beginning to emerge.[7]

So then, this call to radical theology concentrates on those primal figures of modernity who have already voyaged in theologically radical directions—if only theologians would take up the challenge of their example. The philosophers who figure most prominently in this volume—Hegel, Nietzsche, and Heidegger—are those who, in Altizer's sight, can best teach contemporary theologians how to theologize in a radical vein. But also treated here secondarily—as counterexamples to Altizer's own kenotic thinking of God—are recent French philosophers whose "turn to religion," in his view, has been directed in a theologically conservative direction. These include Lacan, Levinas, Derrida, and Marion, whose thinking evokes "that absolutely primordial which is absolute ground and source" (88). Altizer considers Lacan's Phallus, Levinas's Infinite, and Marion's God-without-Being to be evocations "wholly opposed to any possible self-negation or self-emptying" of the sort that Simone Weil, by stark contrast, envisions in her neo-Jansenist religious thinking (chaps. 7 and 8).

In the course of this manifesto Altizer puts forward several positions that may be judged unpalatable from a mainstream point of view: to wit, the notion that Hegel is not *really* an absolute idealist, that Nietzsche *really* is a theologian, that the genuine theologian "speaks for others" and "speaks for all," and does so in the context of a "universal horizon" (though this stance may appear more appreciable in light of Alain Badiou's book on the universalism of Paul).[8] Such counter-mainstream claims deserve to be examined with fresh consideration. But the most potentially off-putting stance of Altizer is his enthusiastic embrace of *apocalypse*, understood as bearing a positive valance. Given the dark brew of associations that the word "apocalypse" stirs in popular imagination, ranging from visions of David Koresh and the Branch Davidians, to film clips of 9/11, to the hyperbolic passions of Christian millennialists, why would a critical theologian seize so insistently on this unsympathetic term?

Altizer employs "apocalypse" to name the historically unprecedented and cataclysmic transformations that have constituted modernity, engulfing us exteriorly while opening up an abyss of unknowing within. He maintains that we late moderns have achieved little understanding of apocalypticism's power and meaning, despite the fact that so many of the primal modern thinkers, including Hegel, Marx, and Nietzsche, have been manifestly apocalyptic thinkers.

> Indeed, the very advent of modernity can be understood to be an apocalyptic event, an advent ushering in a wholly new world as the consequence of the ending of an old world. Nowhere was such a new world more fully present than in thinking itself, a truly new thinking not only embodied in a new science and a new philosophy, but in a new reflexivity or introspection in the interiority of self-consciousness. . . . Cartesian philosophy could establish itself only by ending scholastic philosophy, and with that ending a new philosophy was truly born, and one implicitly if not explicitly claiming for itself a radically new world. That world can be understood as a new apocalyptic world, one which becomes manifestly apocalyptic in the French Revolution and German Idealism, and then one realizing truly universal expressions in Marxism and in that uniquely modern or postmodern nihilism which was so decisively inaugurated by Nietzsche's proclamation of the death of God.[9]

Violent and disruptive transformations, increasingly global in their reach, have constituted our actual history; as such they have fissured and transformed not only our common history but ourselves, our core identities, and not only our core identities but that which we (formerly immanent in our identities) knew and identified as God. Increasingly less able to trace our identities through patterns discernable in the past-unto-the-present, we are flung away from that past, divorced from it, unanchored. Now comprehensive reality as we encounter it is absolute transformation, dislodged from all stabilizing orders and identities. For

Nietzsche, as for Heidegger in his wake, the death of God brings forth an abyss of nihilism, a collapse of European values and a "monstrous logic of terror," but this is intimately connected with a radical, epochal openness—truly a millennial openness.[10]

Nietzsche and Heidegger alike saw their epoch as ending the Christian era and opening an era as yet molten and unnamed. So Altizer likewise emphasizes that apocalypse not only puts an end to the old, it catalyzes the utterly new, creating an opportunity (*portus* = access, port) for transfiguration, for all things breaking away from the known, the given, and becoming transformed: a newness of the world that signals as well the newness of an unnamed anonymous God and the newness of ourselves. Thus Altizer understands the world-transfiguration of our time as the apocalypse of world, humanity, and God in one overwhelming coup of absolute transformation. God is no longer in "heaven" or anywhere transcendent or apart but is—if anywhere—*here*, caught up in this transfigured "chaosmos" of a neither-immanent-nor-transcendent reality. He insists that it is "no longer possible to speak of God in a classical theological language, or any form thereof, and this means that God can no longer be conceived as transcendent or immanent, either as 'above' or 'below,' in the 'heights' or in the 'depths.'"[11] When transcendence is emptied, immanence loses its dichotomous other, hence its otherness, and the demand for a categorically new thinking is upon us (see top of 142).[12]

Confronted with such apocalyptic disruption, conservative Christians continue to assert that God abides in transcendence to the world. While fundamentalists insist that Jesus, the Son of God, was crucified, rose from death in resurrection, and literally ascended in the flesh to the right hand of the Father in heaven, considerable numbers of more sophisticated conservative Christians, including members of the Radical Orthodoxy movement, also continue to maintain the transcendence of God, renewing traditional arguments in a new context. At the opposite extreme, meanwhile, secularists and atheists, including the "new atheists" (Dawkins, Hitchens, Harris, and others), eagerly embrace Nietzsche's core message of the death of God and assume that the demise of God renders crucifixion moot, a fossil symbol emptied of all religious power and meaning.

Altizer, in contrast to both positions, forges the death of God into a radical theology offensive to both camps: a post-theistic theology too ontologically transformative of God (unto Death) for the religious conservative, on the one hand, and too religious in its portent for the strict secularist or atheist on the other. Altizer advocates the live option of a *Christian atheism* as against the options of a God resolutely without atheism or an atheism resolutely without God. While this approach certainly cannot be said to "mediate" the former positions, it does propose an entirely alternative way that conjoins a genuine atheism with a genuine theism. As the reviewer Robert S. Oventile has put it, even a secularist who is indifferent to religion may consider God's death apocalyptic, because for millennia the Occident has been pervaded by the belief that a transcendent eternal being anchors existence: "For both the Christian and the non-Christian, when God dies, an actual nothingness remains."[13]

An atheism that is simply dismissive of God has no capacity to contend with the potency of this actual nothingness—the dark night of nihilism that is effecting a de-foundational disorientation of Western and even global culture; meanwhile, a theism that is ultimately dismissive of atheism tends to discount its actuality altogether, declaring the death of God to be a self-refuting surd, since—if there is a God—by definition God cannot die. Complicating this either/or picture, however, secular theorists and historians are increasingly documenting the religious underpinnings and theological presuppositions that "secularity" has retained—to the point that this has become a mainstream view. Among such theorists, Santiago Zabala defines secularization as "the appropriate way of bearing witness to the attachment of modern European civilization to its own religious past, a relationship consisting not of surpassing and emancipation alone, but conservation, too."[14] He asserts that secularization has become the norm for *all* theological discourse. Another cultural critic, Michael Allen Gillespie, makes patent that even if our age is defined by the death of God, it is still defined by its relationship to God and therefore defined theologically, even if by a negative theology; he argues that secularism itself can be understood as an extreme expression of the concealment of God, the *deus absconditus*, of Protestantism.[15]

But it is not possible to characterize Altizer's death of God theology as expressing a "concealment" of God; it is far rather a full epiphany of the actual negation of God. The God whom we encounter in modernity, Altizer argues, is never essentially God's Being but that Being poured out, evacuated, crucified in a movement of self-emptying that constitutes the genesis of our actual world, permeated by an actual nothingness. This theology centers on kenosis and passion as the essential self-defining acts of Godhead, a kenosis and passion not limited to Jesus but understood to be the passion or kenotic self-negation of Godhead itself, a passion that thus negatively affirms the active Godhead of God, which a flatly irreligious secularist would not accept. This God of universal passion extends life to all the living, a life not rescued from death but grounded in death, for there is no actual life apart from such grounding in death, just as there is no genesis apart from negation. The self-emptying God, who is not the "plenitude of Being" but rather the manifest voiding of that plenitude, is the foundation of existence. Onto-theology is transformed into nihil-theology. Although primordially God is *esse ipsum*, Being itself, existentially God is *becoming Nothing*, the actual perishing of that Being.

Thus we begin to make sense of the crucial contrast Altizer draws here and elsewhere between the "primordial" and the "apocalyptic" Godhead (chaps. 3 and 8). God conceived as pure Being, *ipsum esse subsistens*, is a God untouched by actuality, a God untransformed and untransformable, a perfect quiescence before and apart from creation and incarnation. The apocalyptic God shatters that quiescence, empties Being, crucifying the primordiality of God. This means that the "God after God" (the apocalyptic God) is no longer identifiable as a "God beyond God" (the primordial God) except qua crucified; that is, insofar as crucifixion reconciles these opposites in a *coincidentia oppositorum*. God as Omega is identical to God as Alpha crucified, thus manifesting the self-embodying will of Alpha in creation and incarnation. Granted the fact of incarnation, there can be no return to the primordial God, for the birth of actuality, the creation of an actual world, has wrought an irreversible shattering of Alpha by Omega. This "traumatic core of the divine kenosis," as Žižek characterizes Altizer's position, "retains a properly apocalyptic shattering power" that goes beyond the mere deconstruction of human ideas of God.[16] It is not an all-too-human construct of God that is shattered—an idolatrous faith or an ontotheology—it is God as Being itself that is shattered, giving rise to a universal actuality that is Perishing itself.

The concept of actuality as a "perishing" that is identical to the self-negation of God only fully entered Altizer's theological vocabulary mid-career, with *The Self-Embodiment of God* (1977), as the influence of Hegel became increasingly decisive for his thinking. Altizer's Hegelian understanding of actuality as perishing—which he also names with the phrase "history as apocalypse"—is the core of his dialectical theology, but this is a Hegelian inspiration wholly permeated by Nietzschean nihilism. The actual death of God is not possible in Hegel, as D. G. Leahy observes: given that the beginning of God is not essentially historical (as it is for Altizer), the absolute cannot actually die.[17] Because Altizer renders the historical genesis of God the first actual apocalyptic act of God, it becomes possible for the death of God to be "the actual death of the Godhead not merely the eternal death of an absolute self-consciousness"; as a consequence, now "for the first time in history the non-being of the finite nothingness is the *groundless* infinite."[18] Altizer's thinking grasps actuality (time, history, life) as the continual negation or perishing of an original eternal presence or eternal now (*nunc stans*) that is the primordial God.

Leahy observes that this thinking of absolute ending in Altizer's theology constitutes simultaneously an absolute beginning: because this marks the "absolute and final *end* of every ground of past theology," this "Nothing is the *beginning* of the groundless non-being of the unique God."[19] It is negation in the form of perishing that makes possible an actual beginning or genesis of God and of world alike. Altizer writes, "Genesis or absolute beginning is the perishing of that eternity; it is a beginning which is the perishing or death of an original eternity or totality. . . . Eternity itself becomes absolutely new in that perishing."[20] Altizer thinks through the final and irrevocable death of God, Leahy observes, in effect by eliminating the a priori distinction in Hegel between the for-itself and the in-itself, so that finally "the for-itself is absolutely in-itself the absolute totality of existence."[21] The perishing of God not only generates here-and-now universal actuality, it is identical to it. Actuality *is* the ongoing perishing/beginning of an actual non-being of God by way of the kenotic negation of the inactual primordial being of God. So death or final negation actualizes the "life" of God in the form of perishing, the perpetuation of a universal actual nothingness. Altizer names this actuality the "apocalypse of God."

Altizer's affirmation of incarnation as perishing is indeed traumatic, and conservative or traditional Christians are inclined to ask, what has become of the "good news" that Christianity brought into the world two millennia ago? His answer to this challenge is dialectical, expressed in the light-in-darkness symbolism of the prologue to the Fourth Gospel (John 1:5–9). For Altizer the unique calling of theology is "a calling to voyage into our most absolutely negative depths" (5), into the deepest darkness, yet even as we descend into the apocalyptic "darkness which is now engulfing us" in the wake of the death of God, he insists, the light is not overcome but dialectically revealed:

> Truly epic descents into darkness are simultaneously or inevitably ascents into light, a light whose splendor and glory is a full reversal of the depths and abyss of darkness. Therefore a Christian epic movement into darkness is finally and necessarily a movement into light, as the depths of darkness are here a darkness fully visible, and a darkness truly opening the actual possibility of an apocalyptic day. (121)

Altizer is confident that the threat of annihilating darkness is best dealt with by advancing straight into it with eyes open, rather than evading, denying, or repressing its power and reality as countless "healthy-minded" theologies do. The deepest darkness is a touchstone, manifesting that light is real, not illusion. The strength of a pure theological nihilism of this kind is precisely that it eliminates the escape routes of illusion ("cheap grace") and denial ("bad faith"), both forms of hypocrisy all too evident in many contemporary manifestations of Christianity. Any "good news" or salvation that is premised on the denial, discounting, or neglect of actual misery, oppression, cruelty, injustice, death—crucifixion in all its forms—is at bottom a Gnostic rather than a genuinely Christian gospel. Incarnation entails an actual descent into hell, and crucifixion itself is therein the fount of life, the apocalyptic birth of actual existence.

Throughout his career Altizer has sought to integrate systematic and biblical-historical theology. To achieve this, his overarching strategy has been to trace the historical correlation of modern apocalypticism with the apocalypticism of the early Jesus movement and its ancient anticipations and influences (see chap. 2). Modern apocalypticism is here understood to constitute a rediscovery and reassertion of the apocalypticism originally pervading primitive Christianity at its core, only to be diametrically inverted, reversed, and put under powerful erasure by a Hellenistic and Constantinian Christianity. The apocalyptic event announced by Jesus—God's Kingdom here and now erupting as a living power of *metanoia* and transformation—was rapidly transfigured over a few generations into a transcendent and immutable realm, and by the sixth century CE, Jesus the crucified apocalypticist himself was reversed into Christ the King, Lord of Lords, Pantocrator.

No transformation of a new religious world has been more total or more comprehensive than that which occurred in the first three generations of Christian history, and if primitive Christianity is truly apocalyptic, Hellenistic Christianity becomes fully non-apocalyptic, and this despite its origin in a genuinely apocalyptic Pauline Christianity. Throughout Christian history, apocalyptic movements have been the most subversive movements, and most subversive to all given or established Christianity. While this is true in Judaism and Islam as well, it is only Christianity that has realized a total apocalypticism, as first decisively manifest in medieval Joachism, a Joachism that is deeply reborn in the modern world. (18)

Although Christian apocalypticism resurfaces in earlier historical figures, from Joachim through Hegel, Altizer gives primary credit to the later Nietzsche for fully unveiling the absolute reversal that Christianity effected upon Jesus, inasmuch as Nietzsche described true Christianity—the one practiced by Jesus alone (*Anti-Christ* §39)—as a teaching of the absolute abolition of sin and the advent of blessedness as the only reality (chap. 9). It was precisely his cognizance of the death of God that allowed Nietzsche to discover and unveil this "Buddhist" Jesus who knows no sin or evil, who teaches no God or religion or church whatsoever; who preaches no reward for suffering, no need for redemption after death; but only a divine blessedness already fully realized in this life. This Jesus—Nietzsche's purely "blessed" evangelical Jesus—seals and delivers with finality the death of the Christian God, for such a God of judgment and eternal retribution can no longer be imagined to be real, believed in, or desired—even by "his only Son."

There can be little doubt that the God whom Nietzsche knew to be dead is the uniquely Christian God, but this God who is known in Christianity is a consequence of a radical de-eschatologizing of the original Christian kerygma, or an ultimate transformation of an original apocalyptic Christianity into Hellenistic Christianity, one entailing not only a profound transformation of Jesus, but a transformation of the apocalyptic Kingdom of God that Jesus enacted and embodied into an absolutely sovereign and absolutely transcendent God. (90–91)

Hereafter, post-Nietzsche, the transcendence of God can only be manifest as a repressive or "Satanic" power. Accordingly, the ninth chapter of Nietzsche's *Thus Spoke Zarathustra* addresses those who preach eternal life and renunciation of the world as "preachers of death." To the extent that this God is not apocalyptically dissolved *qua* dead and unreal it persists as the "dead Body of God," a negative power overshadowing the immediacy of life with its alien judgment and attachment to an "eternal life" that is truly anti-life.[22]

So the non-apocalyptic Christian is necessarily conservative, standing with and upholding a status quo ante, whether moderately or overwhelmingly so. The apocalyptic Christian, by contrast, prays and speaks and acts with the conviction that the Kingdom of God is a revolutionary event that is effecting transformation here and now in the world: "Just as the orthodox God is an ever more fully primordial God, the heretical Christian God is an ever more fully eschatological God" (37). The apocalyptic God is self-transfiguring through self-sacrifice—a forward-moving process of dialectical dying-and-birthing, perishing-and-creating—as the newness of the world supplants the old world of the old God and old Adam alike. Because Godhead has become thoroughly actual and historical, the world is born ever anew *ex abysso*.

Thus Altizer can affirm, "while in our world [traditional] theological language is our most enslaving language, it is just thereby that a reversal of our dominant theological language can lead to liberation" (140). Implied here is a liberation of theology from a Gnosticizing tendency of orthodox doctrine to undo the movement of incarnation: that means, a liberation from the classical Christian doctrine that has protected Godhead from the absolute price of incarnation. This liberation is achieved by reversing the Hellenistic doctrine that declares Godhead eternally impassible and immutable.[23] In Altizer's theology, it is the crucifixion that realizes the absolute mutability of Godhead unto Death; the Christian "good news" emanates from this Death on the cross, from the depths of suffering and perishing, where the self-embodying God says Yes to life in the flesh by perishing in the flesh.

Of course this theological stance is unbridled heresy to an orthodox Christian—the recrudescence of the Patripassian heresy that was decisively defeated by the close of the fourth century. For the orthodox believer, God's plenitude of being means that God remains unchanged from the beginning and eternally, hence God is incapable by definition of perishing or suffering or being touched by death or change. Altizer's position, reversing the orthodox, opens the possibility of a God of becoming, a God of absolute newness, one who shatters the primordial state of affairs and breaks out of aseity in self-transfiguration. Altizer calls upon Blake and Hegel as primary modern witnesses to this "self-annihilation of God":

> Only the pure and total reversal of [Jesus's] Kingdom made possible the renewal of the absolutely primordial God, an absolutely primordial God who perishes or dies or is wholly transfigured with the advent of the absolutely new. Initially, this death is most purely enacted by Blake and Hegel as apocalyptic enactors of an absolutely new apocalypse, and this absolutely new apocalypse is a profound renewal of the eschatological Jesus, thus a renewal of that Kingdom of God that Jesus enacted and proclaimed. Nowhere does such a renewal occur in Christian theology, or in the dominant expressions of that theology, but this is a theology that is a deeply non-apocalyptic or non-eschatological theology, a theology centered upon the absolutely primordial Creator, and therefore centered upon an absolutely sovereign and absolutely transcendent Godhead. (37)

Altizer's call to radical theology is a call to envision a Godhead who wills absolute transformation—an actual Life—as against a Godhead who remains eternally self-identical and inactual. It is a call, as well, for a sort of intra-Christian poetic justice inasmuch as the death of the immutable God of orthodoxy "reverses the reversal" of Jesus's Kingdom of God that was effected historically by the Christian church. Or, as Altizer puts this in interrogative form: "Can this uniquely modern enactment, the death of God, be understood as a genuine negation and reversal of that uniquely primordial Godhead realized by a reversal of Jesus's Kingdom of God?" (38).

Here lies the thickest fray of Altizer's battle: to posit the venture of Godhead as a forward-moving enterprise in and toward an actuality that is not "heavenly" but our own, here in real time, and yes, erupting in a vale of Perishing without the option to "return" to a terror-free zone of ontological security.

> When Godhead is deeply and ultimately apprehended as primordial Godhead, the only way to that Godhead is the way of *return*, finally the way of eternal return, one that was ever more fully realized in ancient Christianity and that ever more fully distanced itself from every possible eschatological way, every possible eschatological ground, including that eschatological ground that had been the original ground of Christianity. (37)

Fully launched as we are into the third millennium, an epoch of quantum physics and infinite universe(s), is the time overdue for a new understanding of God and a fresh thinking of ontology? Some of us, though still a minority, think so. In his recent critique of Radical Orthodoxy's call for a "robust ontology" centered on the *analogia entis* of Thomas Aquinas, Adam Kotsko states his objection in these terms:

> One of the blind alleys we need to avoid is this question of the *analogia entis*, this whole typology of the various ontologies and their various levels of robustness. That line of conversation is directed firmly toward the past. . . . It is *by definition* directed toward the unchanging and the unchangingly known. That such an ontology has been believed to be compatible with and necessary for Christianity is undeniable; that Christianity can survive after its eclipse is still uncertain. Yet its eclipse seems to me to be a simple fact. If this conversation is to be a matter of ontology—and on some level this is surely unavoidable—then it must be an ontology that starts from where we are. Rather than railing against modern ontologies for failing to describe a world that is long dead, perhaps one should engage the challenging and thankless task of actually *developing* an ontology that will be credible to us, precisely *us*, here, now, today.[24]

Altizer would concur with the contention that we need an ontology that "starts from where we are" precisely because, in his analysis, where we are is a wholesale negation of every previous historically given ontology.

The theological-ontological status quo ante is utterly dissolved by the death of God, like it or not, and no amount of assertion to the contrary can reverse this actuality.

Given the still-dominant tendency within Christianity to privilege a past-bound ontology, this backward-looking conservatism is what Altizer has contested most fiercely as a fully systematic radical theologian. He maintains, "we can surely know our manifest theologies as backward-moving theologies . . . which must be reversed" (135). The mainstream Christian call to conservatism occurs on two collusive levels of nostalgia, human and divine: that is, nostalgia for established "traditions" and nostalgia for a God who remains immutable *ab origine*. Altizer characterizes the latter nostalgia for God as a yearning for unbeginning or unbirth, one that is finally directed against creation or beginning itself: "Our nostalgia is finally directed against the Creator, for it seeks a plenum which is on the yonder side of creation, and that is the very plenum which perished when 'God said.'"[25] When Augustine prays to his God, "Call us back to yourself. . . . Are there not many who return to you from a deeper pit of darkness . . . ?" we are given to understand our existence in this world, our trajectory through time, as an *exitus*, a movement *away from God*.[26] But this is a Neoplatonic assumption that the Jesus whom we encounter in the gospels patently did not make in announcing the Kingdom of God. Altizer seeks to reconceive theology on the ontologically "groundless" eschatological ground that was the original ground of Christianity—that is, a movement *forward* into the Kingdom of God that is at once dawning and not yet. Why would we pine backward to "find God" when our supreme task is to live forward as creators of an apocalyptic Kingdom aborning here and now?

While Altizer resorts primarily to philosophers for logical and ontological rethinking of God, it is to poets and writers that he turns for resources to imagine a Christian apocalypse incarnate. In *History as Apocalypse* (1985), he first documented what he identifies as "the Christian epic tradition," tracing continuities and transfigurations from Dante to Milton to Blake to Joyce. These epic writers, above all the latter two, are cited repeatedly here in their capacity to provide incomparable inspiration for radical theology through imaginative vision. What distinguishes Christian epic from every other epic, Altizer remarks, is that its voyage occurs "in an interior world that is a historically actual world, a world born in the absolutely new mimesis of Dante's *Inferno* and culminating in the absolutely prosaic mimesis of Joyce's *Finnegans Wake*" (122). He understands each Christian epic as a renewal of its predecessor, in a sense "recreating" its predecessor in a historically new world. This epic recreation enacts a sort of Kierkegaardian repetition of the Christian journey that, in being both interior and historical, reenvisions the Christian cosmos, damnation and salvation, sin and grace, in new images in the context of a new cosmos entirely unknown before—and does this in an eschatological forward movement "so as to finally realize apocalypse" (122).

So, in this call to radical theology Altizer is intent to persuade us, in the spirit of Joyce's Here Comes Everybody, that theology is for everyone and everyone has the implicit vocation to pursue theology, if only to find real light in a darkness that is all too real. The critical ultimatum of the God–world dialectic has come to its breaking point in late modernity and there is no avoiding the contesting nihilisms that have resulted, which reduce ultimately to two: the negation of the world by return to an eternal immutable God (matter perishing into Spirit), or the negation of the eternal immutable God by kenosis into the world (Spirit perishing into matter). If this ultimatum is to be put behind us somehow, it can only be put behind by being thought through rather than denied or evaded. Altizer insists that we are impelled to think God by way of our own actual horizon and world, and "even if this will inevitably call forth a *horror religiosus*, that horror is now inescapable for us" (136).

Notes

* Parenthetical citations in this introduction refer to essays in this volume.

1. This introduction is intended as a guide to the essays published here. For a comprehensive introduction to the deep structure of Altizer's theology, see my essay "Theology as the Thinking of Passion Itself," in *Thinking Through the Death of God: A Critical Companion to Thomas J. J. Altizer*, ed. Lissa McCullough and Brian Schroeder (Albany: State University of New York Press, 2004).

2. Theo Hobson, "Rethinking Postmodern Theology," *Modern Believing* 47, no. 3 (July 2006): 10–20.
3. Altizer, *Genesis and Apocalypse: A Theological Voyage Toward Authentic Christianity* (Louisville: Westminster John Knox, 1990), 2.
4. Altizer's Satan-and-Christ dialectic is most fully articulated in *Genesis and Apocalypse*, chap. 11: "Christ and Satan."
5. Although Tillich is often cited as a forerunner of death of God theology, his later *Systematic Theology* retains the conservative theological stance that God is "the power of being in everything and above everything, the infinite power of being" and is "'by himself': he possesses 'aseity'" (Paul Tillich, *Systematic Theology*, 1:236).
6. In addition to other key figures of the death of God movement in the 1960s, who include William Hamilton, Paul van Buren, Gabriel Vahanian, Richard L. Rubenstein, these contemporaries would include Mark C. Taylor, Robert P. Scharlemann, Charles E. Winquist, Carl Raschke, Theodore W. Jennings, David E. Klemm, David Jasper, D. G. Leahy, and a wide informal network of their students and associates, though this list is certainly not exhaustive. Jeffrey W. Robbins, formerly a student of Winquist, has called for a "nondogmatic" theology that might be secular or religious, with or without God, in his *In Search of a Non-Dogmatic Theology* (Aurora, CO: Davies Group, 2004).
7. A first example of this is Žižek's citation of Altizer in his chapter, "Dialectical Clarity versus the Misty Conceit of Paradox," in *The Monstrosity of Christ: Paradox or Dialectic*, ed. Creston Davis (Cambridge, MA: MIT, 2009), 260–62, a passage of which is cited later. A helpful overview of Žižek's atheist theology, including its close affinities with Altizer, is Adam Kotsko, *Žižek and Theology* (London: T and T Clark, 2008). As recently as 2007, Vattimo indicated that he knew little of Altizer's work, in John D. Caputo and Gianni Vattimo, *After the Death of God*, ed. Jeffrey W. Robbins (New York: Columbia University Press, 2007), 91–92. See also Vattimo's *After Christianity*, trans. Luca D'Isanto (New York: Columbia University Press, 2002) and *Belief*, trans. Luca D'Isanto and David Webb (Stanford: Stanford University Press, 1999). A comparative essay by Matthew E. Harris, "Gianni Vattimo and Thomas J. J. Altizer on the Incarnation and the Death of God: A Comparison" (*Minerva: An Internet Journal of Philosophy* 15 [2011]: 1–19), is in fact focused on Vattimo and weak on Altizer,

as the latter's mature work—nearly a dozen books published since 1970—is unaccountably ignored. Dutch-Belgian scholar Frederiek Depoortere engages Žižek and Vattimo while apparently oblivious to the American stream of death of God thinking in his *The Death of God: An Investigation into the History of the Western Concept of God* (London: T and T Clark, 2007).

8. Alain Badiou, *Saint Paul: The Foundation of Universalism*, trans. Ray Brassier (Stanford: Stanford University Press, 2003).

9. Altizer, "Apocalypticism and Modern Thinking," *Journal for Christian Theological Research* 2, no. 2 (1997): par. 1–27, quote in par. 1; http://www.apu.edu/~CTRF/jctr.html. See also "Modern Thought and Apocalypticism," in *Encyclopedia of Apocalypticism*, vol. 3: *Apocalypticism in the Modern Period and the Contemporary Age*, ed. Stephen Stein, 325–59 (New York: Continuum, 1998).

10. Michael Allen Gillespie, *The Theological Origins of Modernity* (Chicago: University of Chicago Press, 2008), 13.

11. Altizer, "Satan as the Messiah of Nature," in *The Whirlwind in Culture: Frontiers in Theology*, ed. Donald W. Musser and Joseph L. Price (Bloomington: Meyer-Stone Books, 1989), 129.

12. A prevalent misinterpretation claims that Altizer relocates the transcendence of God into a plane of total immanence, producing an undialectical parousia of presence in the world, and unfortunately his choice of the term "total presence" has tended to invite this misinterpretation. I have attempted to correct this, if only briefly, by pointing out that this is the total presence of an *absence* that remains thoroughly dialectical, not only diachronically but synchronically (see "Death of God Reprise: Altizer, Taylor, Vattimo, Caputo, Vahanian," *Journal for Cultural and Religious Theory* 9, no. 3 [Fall 2008]: 105–06; http://www.jcrt.org).

13. Robert S. Oventile, "Let God Die," *Stirrings Still: International Journal of Existential Literature* 1, no. 1 (Fall 2004): 74–82, quote on 76.

14. Santiago Zabala, "A Religion without Theists or Atheists," in Richard Rorty and Gianni Vattimo, *The Future of Religion*, ed. Santiago Zabala (New York: Columbia University Press, 2005), 2.

15. Gillespie, *The Theological Origins of Modernity*, 227. Closely parallel to Gillespie, William Franke argues that secularism has been created through a "transfer" of attributes from God to world: "Secularism, as the declaration of the self-subsistent autonomy of the

world, consists in the transfer of a certain logical and metaphysical structure of self-groundedness from God to the world. . . . The irony here is that in order to be godless the world must itself in effect become God, the unconditioned—the be-all and end-all that is in and for itself" (William Franke, "The Deaths of God in Hegel and Nietzsche," *Religion and the Arts* 11 [2007]: 214–41, quote on 219). Gillespie uses the word "transference" to express this same idea (273).

16. Žižek, "Dialectical Clarity versus the Misty Conceit of Paradox," 260.

17. D. G. Leahy, *Foundation: Matter the Body Itself* (Albany: State University of New York Press, 1996), 596. Franke notes that in Hegel, "death is sublated into the infinity of the divine life by God's taking death upon himself," and death is thereby negated and overcome (Franke, "The Deaths of God in Hegel and Nietzsche," 217).

18. Leahy, *Foundation*, 597. The historical beginning or "genesis" of God is the particular focus of Altizer's *The Genesis of God: A Theological Genealogy* (Louisville: Westminster John Knox, 1993).

19. Leahy, *Foundation*, 597, my italics.

20. Altizer, *Genesis and Apocalypse*, 39.

21. Leahy, *Foundation*, 597.

22. Altizer, *Godhead and the Nothing* (Albany: State University of New York Press, 2003), 71, 155–58.

23. For one scholar's argument that divine impassibility and immutability are a purely Greek—or "pagan"—concern imposed upon or read into the biblical texts, see Rem B. Edwards, "The Pagan Dogma of the Absolute Unchangeableness of God," *Religious Studies* 14, no. 3 (Sept. 1978): 305–13.

24. Adam Kotsko, "'That They Might Have Ontology': Radical Orthodoxy and the New Debate," *Political Theology* 10, no. 1 (2009): 115–24, quote on 122.

25. Altizer, *Genesis and Apocalypse*, 104.

26. Augustine, *Confessions*, trans. R. S. Pine-Coffin (New York: Penguin, 1961), 8:4, 163.

1

DOING RADICAL THEOLOGY

Apparently we are now entering an era in which radical theology is simply impossible. It is surely not being taught in any of our theological centers, just as it is unknown to the general public, and seemingly unknown to our professional theologians. A genuine radical theology is not to be confused with our various liberation theologies, all of which are conservative theologically, nor is it to be confused with radical fundamentalism of any kind. For a genuinely radical theology is a theological thinking that truly rethinks the deepest ground of theology, a rethinking that is initially an unthinking of every established theological ground; only through such an unthinking can a clearing be established for theological thinking, and that is the very clearing that is the first goal of radical theology. Nor can this be accomplished by a simple dissolution of our given theological grounds, for those are the very grounds that must here be ultimately challenged, and challenged in terms of their most intrinsic claims. Indeed, this has already decisively occurred, as most clearly manifest in our world by the impossibility of all established theologies to be biblical theologies, or to be biblical theologies incorporating a truly critical understanding of the Bible. This has always been true in all of our neo-orthodoxies, which by necessity phenomenologically suspend all scholarly understanding of the Bible, a bracketing or *epochē* impelled by a uniquely modern situation, a condition in which there is no possibility of integrating anything that we can know as faith with anything that we can critically understand. Nothing has more challenged our theologies than biblical scholarship, and this is true in all our theological worlds, and while once biblical scholars could be genuinely theological, now theology has virtually disappeared from our biblical criticism and scholarship.

Unfortunately this is a situation that seemingly makes a critical or even a genuine theology impossible, and for the first time we are bereft of fully systematic theologies that are critical theologies, and this is above all true of our fundamental thinking of God, which is now our most silent or most forbidden theological topic. But is this a clearing that the radical theologian can not only accept but affirm? Is it possible that such a clearing is now essential to genuine theological thinking? If so, that is not a clearing that can simply be taken for granted, but far rather one that must be theologically thought through, and thought through by theological thinking itself. All too fortunately this has already occurred, and occurred in our greatest modern philosophical theologies, and not the philosophical theologies of modern theologians, but rather those of our most radical modern philosophers, including not only Spinoza and Hegel but also Nietzsche and Heidegger. Simply to mention these philosophers is to evoke a uniquely modern radical theological thinking, one that has not only profoundly rethought the ground or grounds of theology, but has done so only by deeply unthinking every established theological ground. Ironically, it was Spinoza who initiated a truly modern understanding of the Bible, just as it was Hegel who more fully incorporated a biblical ground into his thinking than has any other philosopher, and Nietzsche and Heidegger who fully embodied an apocalyptic horizon in their thinking, one absent from all of our established theologies, and this despite the modern historical discovery of the apocalyptic ground of an original Christianity.

We must be prepared to accept the paradox that modern philosophy has been more deeply theological than modern theology, which is perhaps not so paradoxical if our greatest modern imaginative vision has been more fully theological than has our theological thinking. This is already true of Dante, and in our world it is true of Joyce. But this is a deeply heterodox vision, and one becoming ever more fully heterodox as it evolves, which is exactly the movement that can be discovered in the evolution of modern philosophy, which is why most modern theologians have deeply resisted modern philosophy, a resistance that is a pure opposition in the greatest of all modern religious thinkers, Kierkegaard. Kierkegaard could know modern philosophy as a truly pagan thinking, hence it is not theologically neutral but rather the very opposite of genuine faith. While Kierkegaard absorbed Hegel's dialectical thinking, he inverted it just as did Marx, and it is this inversion that made possible his thinking of the pure subjectivity or deep interiority of faith. Yet this is possible only by way of a profoundly solitary thinking, a solitary thinking only fully paralleled in Nietzsche, which is why Nietzsche can be understood as the polar opposite or dialectical twin of Kierkegaard. Indeed, Nietzsche opposed modern philosophy even more profoundly than did Kierkegaard, although following Heidegger it is possible to understand Nietzsche as the consummation of Western philosophy, and above all so in his ultimate and final realization of the death of God.

That is indeed an apocalyptic realization, one bringing our history to an end, an ending most purely realized in the depths of the late modern imagination, and even as Nietzsche is the philosopher who is most open to those depths, it is Nietzsche who had the greatest philosophical impact upon late modern artists and poets. So it is that Nietzsche can genuinely be known as a poetic philosopher, even as Kierkegaard can be known as a poetic religious thinker, and if here thinking and the imagination are truly united, this is a union that has been impervious to all of our theology. Is a genuinely imaginative theology simply inconceivable, a truly ironic situation in a world that has been given such profoundly theological poetry, music, and art, art truly alien to the world of theology, and above all alien to every theology that is commonly known or manifest. Could this be a genuine way for the contemporary radical theologian? It would surely be a solitary way, but is not solitude essential for the genuinely radical theologian? Certainly no home is now at hand for the radical theologian in our theological or academic worlds, and while radical thinkers seemingly abound among us, radical theologians are virtually invisible, and most others would no doubt respond to radical theology as an oxymoron. Yet it is manifest that great philosophers can be radical theological thinkers, perhaps all of them have been so; is it inconceivable that a thinking in this spirit could occur today?

Now if radical theology is understood as a solitary way, it cannot be an ecclesiastical theology, cannot be bound to any established norms or traditions, and here Kierkegaard is once again a primary model, and his final assault upon the church was a consistent fulfillment of the evolution of his thinking. Here, we can see all too clearly how the deepest religious or theological thinking can be an anti-ecclesiastical thinking, and not only can be but must be an anti-ecclesiastical thinking, or must be so in a genuinely modern world. Not since Leibnitz could a major thinker be an ecclesiastical thinker, and if ours is a world in which ecclesiastical theology is all in all, or all in all in our theological worlds, nothing else has so estranged theology from our world, or so called it forth as a truly alien or archaic thinking. Hence the genuine theologian must now realize a new solitude, a solitude that is perhaps unique to the theologian today, nothing comparable to this solitude would appear to occur in other worlds of thinking, there are no academies or associations for the real theologian in our world, as witness the theological poverty of the American Academy of Religion, or the near collapse of genuine theological publishing or truly theological periodicals. For an enormous transformation has occurred in only a single generation, one comparable to the transformation of our political world, and just as only conservative politicians now seem to be actually possible, only conservative theologians are now manifest among us, and they inspire as little respect as do our politicians.

Genuinely radical theological thinking has always been an offensive thinking, and most offensive to the larger community of faith, or to an established religious world. So if such thinking were to occur today it would inevitably create an offense, and here, too, theological thinking is unique in our world. Who could imagine a poet or a philosopher creating an offense today? We even lack truly offensive politicians, or genuinely offensive public figures, and while many can respond to our world as the best of all possible worlds, it is apparently not open to an ultimate challenge of any kind. Yet this is precisely the calling of the radical theologian, for the radical theologian is dedicated to an ultimate challenge to our deepest ground, and even if such a ground is now seemingly unnameable, it is necessarily called forth in a truly radical theological thinking. Clearly such thinking cannot simply challenge the Church or challenge society, it must go far deeper than that, for it is inevitably a challenge to everything that we can know or name as God, or anything whatsoever with an absolute claim. But how is this possible today? Does it call for a stepping out from every community, and one not simply realizing a genuine solitude, but a truly new solitude, one only possible in our new world? Again, Spinoza, Kierkegaard, and Nietzsche are genuine models, for each not only realized a truly new solitude, but that solitude was absolutely essential to their thinking, and it made possible a new and liberating solitude for innumerable others.

Here, too, theological thinking differs from other thinking in our world, for it is inseparable from an intention to address the world at large, and even if this should occur only fragmentarily, it is nevertheless essential to theological thinking itself, and essential to the deepest life of the theologian. While that life may well be a truly solitary life, it can never be a private life, can never be divorced from the vocation of the theologian, for that calling is as ultimate as any other, and is perhaps unique in foreclosing every possibility of a private haven or ground. If only at this point, Nietzsche is a genuine theologian, for even if many are totally committed to their work or calling, it is perhaps the theologian alone who is truly homeless, and homeless if only because he or she must so ultimately challenge every possible Home or Haven. Thus the theologian is by necessity called to an exploration of the truly or even the absolutely negative, that pure negative that is the deepest challenge to all life, and which theologically is known as an eternal death or damnation. While damnation ever more progressively disappeared from modern theology as opposed to all previous Christian theology, it has truly been renewed not only in the horrors of our world but in the deepest imaginative enactments of the late modern world, enactments alien to all of our contemporary philosophy, but truly essential to genuine theology today. This, too, is a unique calling of theology, a calling to voyage into our most absolutely negative depths, a voyage apart from which theology could only be truly vacuous.

Yes, the theologian is a voyager, and above all so the radical theologian, but a voyager into the deepest darkness, a voyage apart from which every voyage into light is now wholly empty and unreal. How can the theologian become open to such darkness? First, this can occur only when every safety net has been removed, only when our innermost center is truly naked and alone, and we fully open ourselves to that absolute abyss that then inevitably engulfs us. While each of us is standing over an abyss, it is the theologian who is called to name that abyss, and to name it with an ultimate or absolute name, that name of names which is the name of God or the Godhead, and which here can be manifest only as an absolute abyss. And as opposed to every apophatic or negative theology, or every mystical theology, this is an absolute abyss that is absolutely actual as that abyss, absolutely actual as a pure negativity, and absolutely actual not in an absolutely primordial horizon, but far rather in that horizon which is absolutely here and now. Hence a genuine Christianity has always known an absolute judgment, a total judgment inseparable from every possible joy, and if the theologian as opposed to the artist has only falteringly named joy, he or she can fully name judgment, and the fuller the theologian the fuller the naming of judgment and abyss. So it is that every genuine theology is a truly negative theology, and every genuine theologian a truly negative theologian, a negative theology inseparable from the most ultimate offense, and inseparable from a profound laceration that is the inevitable consequence of a genuinely theological calling.

Thus there are no innocent theologians, or none who are genuine theologians, for the theologian inevitably embodies that sickness which Kierkegaard knew as the sickness unto death, a sickness that is not only an ultimate *Angst*, but a sickness in which an actual nothingness or an actual abyss is here wholly embodied or enfleshed. Theological thinking is inevitably a pathological thinking, or surely so in our world, and if once again this is truly distinctive of theological thinking, a theological calling is a calling to an ultimate darkness, and a darkness truly visible in our new world. Yet if it is visible, and hearable, too, it is apparently unnameable, or perhaps nameable only theologically, for if theological naming is unique in naming an absolute darkness and an absolute abyss, then certainly there is an ultimate necessity for theological naming today. However, such naming can occur only through an incorporation of that abyss which it names, so it cannot be a vicarious bearing of abyss, nor can it be any form of game or play, for it is inseparable from an actual brokenness, an actual brokenness that is a sign or seal of the genuine theologian. Why then would anyone accept or choose such a calling? Because for the theologian that brokenness is inseparable from an ultimate joy, an ultimate joy that the theologian names as grace, but a grace inseparable and finally indistinguishable from brokenness itself.

Bonhoeffer is that theologian who most decisively drew forth the utter emptiness of a "cheap grace," a wholly illusory grace that is indeed the very opposite of grace, and even if such grace is a mass phenomenon, it is the grace of "hollow men," a humanity that is human only in its mask. Note how such a humanity is the very opposite of the

Here Comes Everybody of *Finnegans Wake*, an everybody that could only be an embodied everybody, as manifest in the total actuality of its voice. The enactment of an apocalyptic resurrection in the conclusion of *Finnegans Wake* is certainly the enactment of an absolute joy, but an absolute joy that is inseparable from an absolute chaos or an absolute abyss, and here we can decisively understand how a voyage into an absolute abyss is a voyage into an absolute joy. While there are few theological explorations of *Finnegans Wake*, this is nevertheless an apocalyptic epic for all of us, and perhaps that modern epic which most illuminates a theological vocation in our world, which most openly calls forth an ultimate identity of darkness and light. Consequently, a truly theological exploration of absolute darkness is precisely thereby an exploration of absolute light, so that here joy is realized through darkness itself, and if the theologian is enslaved to darkness, that is the theological way of realizing joy itself, and an absolute joy that is possible only through an absolute darkness. Yes, there is a deep joy in doing theology, and the deepest joy in doing the most radical theology, only that theology embodies such a *coincidentia oppositorum*, or embodies a damnation that is redemption itself.

Can the theologian taste such redemption, or is it possible only to know it vicariously? The answer to these questions is immediately manifest, for a vicarious theology is clearly no theology at all. Here, perhaps, theology differs most deeply from philosophy, or differs from every philosophy that is not an absolutely solitary philosophy, or every philosophy that is not finally a theological philosophy. Yes, a genuinely theological thinking is a tasting of redemption, that is the source of its ultimate joy, but this is a joy only realizable through an absolute darkness and abyss, or that very darkness which the theologian embraces in embracing her or his calling. The joy is so deep in this calling that it truly makes possible a solitary way, but a solitary way ultimately directed to the world itself, and to that world that is immediately at hand. Hence a theological language is inevitably a language of witness, and of confession, too, a confession of that absolute guilt which is called forth by the advent of an absolute joy, so this is a witness to guilt and joy at once, and to a joy that is only a "cheap grace" apart from an absolute guilt. Yes, Kierkegaard is our deepest modern theologian, or our deepest theologian who is only a theologian, and as he himself confesses he was called to be an ultimate witness, and a witness even in his all too

actual brokenness and despair, a despair that is the very signature of
a genuine theology, but a despair inseparable from the most absolute
forgiveness.

Now it is not to be forgotten that Kierkegaard was our first thinker
to know an absolute *horror religiosus*, a horror whereby he could know
himself as a second Job, and just as Job is the only ultimate No-sayer to
God in the Bible, Kierkegaard is our only thinker until Nietzsche who
could pronounce an ultimate No upon God. But Kierkegaard is a truly
dialectical thinker, so that his No to God is at bottom an absolute Yes,
and a Yes inseparable from that No, or a Yes inseparable from the most
ultimate *Angst*. Once again we can see how a realization of the most absolute judgment is a realization of the most absolute grace, and this is
a realization that the theologian is called upon not only to explore, but
to realize in his or her ownmost center, a center that is body and soul
at once, or is that body which is a fully embodied center, a center apart
from which theological thinking is vacuous and unreal. Perhaps the
very dominance of a vacuous theological thinking among us is a sign
of a new theological call, a call arising out of this very void, and one
inseparable from that void itself. And inseparable if only because we are
now called upon to realize the greatest possible theological negation, a
negation of every theology that is now manifest as theology, or every
theology immediately nameable as theology today. But this can only
be a theological negation, a negation wherein theology negates itself,
a self-negation that is a self-emptying, and a self-negation of ultimate
ground itself.

Here, Hegel is the supreme philosophical master, that Hegel who
has given us the only absolute philosophy of self-negation, or the only
one in the West, a self-negation that is an absolute self-emptying, and
an absolute self-emptying embodying the Crucified God. Hegel is the
first philosopher of the death of God precisely as a profoundly Christian thinker, that thinker who first actually thought the Crucifixion, a
thinking revolutionizing philosophy, a revolution that for Hegel is a
decisive sign of the advent of the third and final Age of the Spirit. Of
course, this originally occurs in the Incarnation and the Crucifixion,
but only now does it occur in thinking itself, a thinking that is the
consummation of philosophy, and a consummation of world history
itself. Hence Hegel is a truly apocalyptic thinker, but so likewise are his
reverse descendents, Nietzsche and Heidegger, and it is only in Hegel,
Nietzsche, and Heidegger that philosophical and historical thinking are

truly conjoined. Inevitably, this is a radical theological thinking, the most heterodox theological thinking that has ever occurred, but only now has the occasion arisen to mediate that thinking to theological thinking as a whole. While that could only be a profound subversion of theology, that is a death that promises life, and promises life to theology itself, or to that theology which is capable of undergoing a resurrection through an ultimate and final death. Indeed, this is the path of the radical theologian today, a path of ultimate subversion that is just thereby a resurrection of theology itself. Although this is a path calling forth multiple ways, it is a path in which an absolute negation and an absolute affirmation are inseparable, and inseparable in that thinking which is a genuine theological thinking.

In this perspective, Hegel can certainly be known as a theological thinker, and Nietzsche, too, and here the deepest negation is the deepest affirmation, an absolute affirmation finally indistinguishable from an absolute negation. Is this a thinking that can be communicated to the world at large? Surely not in its Hegelian form, but perhaps in its Nietzschean embodiment, and above all so if that embodiment could be realized in a common language, or in a language understandable to all. Yet this has always been the mission of theology, to speak the absolute in the language of everybody, and to speak it in such a way that one immediately responds, and responds to that which one hears as our ultimate ground. Nor can we deny the enormous success of theology in this endeavor, at least in the Western world; even today the majority of humanity embrace such a theology, a majority that seemingly can speak the name of God without embarrassment or hesitation. Of course, this can no longer occur in our critical discourse, but it did so occur for almost two millennia, as theological language was the most powerful language throughout that period, and even political sovereignty could not then be separated from theological sovereignty. Yes, Christendom has come to an end, as Kierkegaard was the first to know, but does not a theological legacy remain that has enormous potential power?

This is a power that the radical theologian seeks, a power to move the world at large; thereby theology is truly unique, and unique in seeking to address in depth the world as a whole. Indeed, this is just the power that a radical transformation of theological language promises, for if that language can remain itself even in this transformation, it will embody such a power and be greeted with ultimate response. Every theologian who is a homoletical theologian knows this well, and if every ultimate proclamation is a theological proclamation, at least in its impact, again we can understand Nietzsche as a theologian, and a theologian who is here a primal guide for a new radical theologian. This is the theologian who can greet Nietzsche's absolute theological negations as being at bottom theological affirmations, affirmations making possible what Nietzsche ecstatically proclaimed as Eternal Recurrence, and an Eternal Recurrence that is certainly a theological Eternal Recurrence, for it promises the most ultimate redemption, and a redemption from the most ultimate guilt and *ressentiment*. Nietzsche could know his world as the emptiest world in history, a world not only foreshadowing our own, but far more fully embodied now than then, yet only such a dark and empty world is open to an apocalyptic proclamation of Eternal Recurrence, or to an apocalyptic Yes. Can such a Yes be pronounced today, and be pronounced so as to be heard? Is this not the mission of theology today, even if it can be realized only in the most radical theology?

Without any question theology is a truly audacious enterprise, and while it is commonly ridiculed as such, it can inspire deep dread, for it certainly can be pathological in its effect, and more universally pathological than any other discourse. This, too, is a decisive sign of its power, and how significant that Heidegger could so fully employ the theological language of fall, guilt, and dread in his greatest work, language inseparable from the ultimate impact of Heidegger, and of that Heidegger who is the only twentieth-century philosopher who came out of a theological vocation and underwent a full theological education. There are few theologians who know as much theology as Heidegger, and none who could so powerfully know authentic existence as "being toward death," a uniquely Christian motif, but one fully explicated only by Heidegger himself. Can the theologian forget what an enormous impact this explication had, or forget that he realized this understanding while at Marburg, where he deeply participated in a New Testament seminar and himself became a master of Paul. This is evidenced already in 1920 in his lectures on the phenomenology of religion, where he identifies Paul as an apocalyptic thinker, which was not discovered by New Testament scholarship until the publication of Schweitzer's great book on Paul in 1927. How can one deny Heidegger as a great theologian, for even if he is silent about God until his posthumously published *Beiträge zur Philosophie* (*Contributions to*

Philosophy), this is a theological silence about God, and one that many theologians have embraced.

All too significantly an ultimate assault upon the Christian God again and again occurs in *Beiträge*, where there is a deep emphasis upon the abandonment of Being, one that first happens in Christianity and its absolutely transcendent God, an abandonment in which Being abandons beings, but this abandonment is the fundamental event in our history, and one that is now being reversed in the apocalyptic advent of *Ereignis*. While *Beiträge* is a much too difficult a book to have a universal impact, its impact could be mediated through a more common language, and this is just the task of the theologian today. For the theologian is a mediator, and a mediator intending to communicate an ultimate language to all and everyone, and even if this entails a transformation of that language, it is just such transformations that have most transformed the world. Even if it is impossible to deny the pathological impact of theology, it can be understood that this is inseparable from the positive impact of theology, an impact wherein theology makes possible an ultimate language for everyone, a language not only confronting but finally blessing our most ultimate ground. Although that ground can be known as an awesome abyss, as it has been known and envisioned in the late modern world, that is an abyss which is inseparable from our deeper life and existence, and which we must speak if we are truly to confront the world, or truly to confront our existence itself. Finally we must say Yes to that abyss, and this has always been the deepest language of theology, and a language that must now be recovered if we are to speak, and speak in a new world of an absolute and universal speechlessness.

Yet how is the theologian to speak this Yes? Is that actually possible today, could it be dialectically possible, could we become open to that Yes by realizing its very opposite, a truly and finally absolute No? Certainly our new condition is open to such a venture, and most manifestly so in our new emptiness, an emptiness harboring a new abyss, and while that abyss is seemingly unspeakable as such, it could be nameable by the theologian, and by that theologian who has accepted a calling to name God, and to name God in her or his world. Is that name speakable today? It surely is so insofar as it evokes an absolute abyss, and that naming has overwhelmingly occurred in the late modern world; one has only to think of Kafka, and of Beckett, as these primal writers are inheritors of an ultimately dark actuality in the modern world, and one that finally and theologically can only be named as God. Perhaps this naming most powerfully occurs in Melville's *Moby-Dick*, and if the White Whale is an absolute nothingness consuming everything in its wake, that all too actual nothingness can only theologically be named as God, a naming that itself is an ultimate source of the namelessness of God in our world. If the theologian is to meet the challenge of naming God in our world, and hence of becoming open to this abyss, this will require an ultimate courage, a courage making possible a voyaging into absolute abyss.

Courage is not a virtue that we commonly ascribe to the theologian, indeed, the very opposite would appear to be true. Is theology not a deeper if not the deepest source of our backward movements and of our purest *ressentiment?* Perhaps no body of thinkers has a more negative image in our world than do theologians, who are certainly scorned in the academic world, treated with condescension if not contempt by our liberal and radical circles, and even largely if not wholly ignored by our churches and synagogues. If radical theologians are exempt from such indifference or contempt, this is simply because we are virtually unknown, but that might give us a freedom that is otherwise unavailable, a freedom to move invisibly in a world alien to our calling without attracting any attention at all. So let us be invisible theologians, wearing whatever mask might be at hand, masks necessary if only to preserve our own sanity, and perhaps masks truly necessary to ourselves, for we are venturing upon an awesome task. Then perhaps the requisite courage will be given us, for even if it is absent in ourselves, we can hope for it as a free gift of grace, and if we know that a genuine grace can only be a free and wholly undeserved grace, that may well be a grace freely given us in our radical calling. For ours is not simply a voyage of our own, it is a voyage for others, and not for an elite body but rather for everyone and everybody, for ours is finally a universal voyage, finally a voyage that will be undergone by all.

Initially, this appears to be an impossible voyage, but let us recall the voyage of the Christian epic tradition, a voyage that always begins by way of an entrance into absolute abyss, and this epic voyage is enacted as a voyage for everyone, for the Christian epic hero is everyman or everybody. So each of us is called to voyage into that abyss, and here the theologian can be no more than a surrogate for others, but we must be a willing surrogate, one who freely accepts this voyage, and does so even knowing its terrible risks and its seemingly devastating consequences. No vicarious participation is possible here, nor could we possibly be simply spectators of this voyage, for this is a voyage that can truly be a voyage only by actually being enacted, and enacted in our own center. That is the center that will be transfigured by this voyage, a transfiguration only possible by an inversion or reversal of ourselves, but that reversal is the very essence of this voyage, so our voyage begins with a sinking into the depths of chaos itself. Little wonder that theology can truly be known to be a pathological way, or an ultimately negative way, but that negation is essential to this calling, for there is no actual way to theological light apart from an immersion in darkness itself. Finally, we must bless the darkness that overwhelms us and ecstatically greet an absolute darkness, for that is the darkness which will finally become light, as epically enacted for us in the uniquely modern epics of Blake and Joyce.

Blake is that ultimate visionary who first dialectically and apocalyptically enacted a *coincidentia oppositorum* between Christ and Satan; this is realized in the culmination of that epic voyage here enacted, but Blake is also our first prophetic visionary of the death of God, and he finally envisioned Satan as the dead body of God. That is the body that is incarnate in a uniquely modern abyss, and that is the body which we initially enter on our voyage, a body which we can know as the White Whale, or as that absolute abyss that a Kafka or a Beckett call forth. So there can be little doubt of its ultimate actuality, but if we can truly know this abyss as the dead and alien body of God, or as that negative pole of the Godhead when it is wholly severed from its contrary or opposite, then we can become open to that absolute Yes which is the absolute opposite of this absolute No. Yet we can become so open only after having passed through that absolute No, hence we must fully and actually know an absolute *horror religiosus* if we are to become open to a final and apocalyptic Yes. Of course, this is the very path of Nietzsche, just as it is of Joyce, but our calling is to open the way of these great visionaries to all and everyone; this we can do only by enacting this voyage ourselves, doing so in the specific world of theology, and doing so in such a way that a path is thereby established for everybody, for we are Here Comes Everybody.

Now if Christianity knows the Crucifixion as the one source of redemption, that is a crucifixion which full modernity knows as an actual and final death of God, a death of God releasing an awesome and absolute emptiness or nothingness, a releasement whose consequence is the advent of an ultimate nihilism. All of us know that nihilism, even if we do so only vicariously, and if that nihilism is an apocalyptic nihilism, if it is the consequence of the ending of our history, it is finally inseparable from an apocalyptic light. We must pass through that nihilism to realize that light, so even theology must become nihilistic today, and just as many of our most astute thinkers know that genuine theology is inseparable from a nihilistic ground, or is finally inseparable from an ultimate dissolution of every historical and cosmic ground, as is fully manifest in our purest mystical theology, then the theologian today must become open to the most ultimate nihilism. Indeed, we cannot enter an absolute chaos and darkness apart from a fully nihilistic ground, apart from knowing absolute nothingness itself, and even as our deeper mystical theologies have ever known an absolute nothingness, and known it as Godhead or *sunyata* itself, we must know our actual nothingness as the body of God, and thus we must inevitably become nihilistic theologians. This may be the very point at which our work is most open to others, for everyone inevitably struggles with nihilism today, even when unable to know it as nihilism, but if theology can call forth a nihilism that finally reverses itself, then even in our world theology could be known as an ultimate blessing.

Yes, our voyage must necessarily take us into the center of nihilism, and we will no doubt incur incurable wounds thereby, but our goal is to pass through that nihilism, or to pass through a wholly alien darkness and abyss. Already our greatest modern visionaries have accomplished this; our task is to accomplish this movement in an all too common way, so that it can be mediated to everyone. Hence our language must be neither abstract nor arcane, it should be exoteric rather than esoteric, written in the *koine* of our world just as was the New Testament itself. While this is an extraordinarily difficult task, and few realize what a miracle the New Testament is at this point, this at least must be our goal, and to the extent that we fall short of it we will have failed theologically. But theological language itself has immense power here, and even as it has been overwhelmingly powerful in the past, it could become so once again, but only if it is a truly and even absolutely new theological language. Again, Blake and Nietzsche could be models for us, for both could employ an immensely powerful language that is immediately understandable, and this despite the fact that scholars will never cease to unravel the intricacies of their texts. Indeed, the most common language ever employed by a prophet was employed by Jesus in his parables, parables that we have finally begun to understand in their overwhelming power, a power that was lost when they were understood as moral or mystical allegories.

Now we know that those parables are parables of the Kingdom of God, hence they are apocalyptic parables, but they are vastly removed from the genre of apocalyptic discourse, distant from all esoteric vision, and they apparently were immediately understandable by their hearers. Could an apocalyptic Yes for us be one that we could immediately understand? Or understand once we have passed through our dark abyss, or perhaps understand even as we are passing though that abyss? Would such a passage be possible apart from some such understanding? If we can actually name our darkness, we can truly stand within it, hence the deep grace of an apocalyptic naming of darkness, for if it is a genuinely apocalyptic naming it is inseparable from an apocalyptic naming of light. An apocalyptic light dawns only in the deepest darkness and is impossible apart from the total realization of that darkness, for the very advent of an apocalyptic darkness is inseparable from the advent of an apocalyptic light. This ultimate truth is fully manifest in all of our truly apocalyptic visionaries and thinkers, and most clearly so in Blake and Nietzsche, so that we are called to greet that absolute darkness which we confront as an absolutely gracious darkness, a darkness inseparable from an absolute Yes. So that this absolute No is inseparable from that Yes, and finally to know this No is to know that Yes, and to embody this No is finally to embody that Yes.

Is this a truth that we can truly know, indeed, is it possible to be open to this truth without knowing it, and actually knowing and actually embodying it? The deepest grace may well be the most immediate grace, that grace which is most actually at hand, but a grace that we inevitably lose when we turn away from that immediacy, a turning that is a universal turning, and one becoming ever more universal as it evolves. So it is that all our deeper religious ways initially call forth a universal darkness or a universal fall, a darkness that is a totality of samsara or sin, but that is the very darkness that is reversed in enlightenment or redemption. Then a redemptive grace is all in all, but this is a grace that is manifest or knowable only insofar as it is embodied, otherwise it is wholly illusory or only a "cheap grace," or a negative grace deepening an unregenerate condition. Now even if a genuinely redemptive grace is an absolutely impossible grace, and absolutely impossible for us, that very impossibility evokes its possibility as grace, and to know that possibility is to know an absolute Yes. And genuinely to hear that Yes is to embody it, so that if we hear that Yes we will embody it, and do so even in a wholly broken condition. Then we can and will say Amen, and say Amen even if we know ourselves to be wholly empty or dead; indeed, it is only the truly dead or the truly empty who can hear that Yes, but in hearing that Yes, death becomes life itself, and even we can not only know but thereby embody resurrection itself, a resurrection that could only be an absolute Yes.

—October 2002

2

ANCIENT AND MODERN APOCALYPTICISM

While apocalypticism is extraordinarily powerful today, there is no common understanding of apocalypticism, nor even a common conception of it among our scholars of apocalypticism. We do know that there are both ancient and modern forms of apocalypticism, with decisive differences between them, and a fundamental way of illuminating apocalypticism would be to investigate these differences, though this has not yet fully or genuinely occurred. There is substantial agreement that apocalypticism originated in ancient Iran, but we have little knowledge of that apocalypticism; it is only in ancient Israel that an apocalypticism is manifest that can be critically investigated. It was the prophetic revolution that released apocalypticism in Israel, and above all so that postexilic prophecy which is so deeply apocalyptic, as most purely embodied in Second Isaiah. But apocalypticism is alien to that rabbinic Judaism which was born in exile, and there is no historical record of apocalypticism after the canonical prophets until the second century BCE. Then apocalypticism is genuinely powerful, one not only called forth in rebellions against an alien Seleucid monarchy, but in the foundation of that truly apocalyptic community which produced the Dead Sea Scrolls, and within a century apocalypticism is even more powerful, culminating from a Christian point of view in the advent of Christianity itself.

Not only did apocalyptic groups expect the immediate coming of the end of the world, but that very expectation called forth a radical way of life, one reversing everything that is given and manifest as the world, and intending even now to embody that new creation or new aeon which is here called forth. The original Christian title of this new creation is "Kingdom of God," and it is noteworthy that this title does not occur in any extant writing until the New Testament, being absent even from the Dead Sea Scrolls. And it is of vital importance not to confuse an apocalyptic kingdom of God with that kingdom of God which is called forth by the Torah, and above all by that Deuteronomic tradition that so decisively influenced postexilic Israel and that later had an overwhelming impact upon Christianity. This is the kingdom of God that is the eternal reign of God, thereby wholly differing from a kingdom of God that is a new creation or new aeon, a new creation only possible by way of the ending of the old creation.

Indeed, no transformation of a new religious world has been more total or more comprehensive than that which occurred in the first three generations of Christian history, and if primitive Christianity is truly apocalyptic, Hellenistic Christianity becomes fully non-apocalyptic, and this despite its origin in a genuinely apocalyptic Pauline Christianity. Throughout Christian history, apocalyptic movements have been the most subversive movements, and most subversive to all given or established Christianity. While this is true in Judaism and Islam as well, it is only Christianity that has realized a total apocalypticism, as first decisively manifest in medieval Joachism, a Joachism that is deeply reborn in the modern world. If Joachim of Fiore is the first truly apocalyptic thinker, his thinking not only profoundly affected the Spiritual Franciscans but also Dante himself, so that Joachim appears as a redeemed and shining prophet in the *Paradiso* (12:140). Perhaps Joachism was most heretical in identifying the Papacy with the Antichrist, but this occurs in Dante too (*Inferno* 9:53), and this is an apocalyptic identification in both Joachism and Dante.

Dante inaugurated the Christian epic tradition, and this tradition has been apocalyptic throughout its history, becoming ever more fully apocalyptic as it evolved, and in Blake apocalypticism becomes total as it had never been before. Moreover, Blake was the first apocalyptic visionary to rediscover the apocalyptic Jesus, or fully to do so, an apocalyptic Jesus who is the very antithesis of the Christ of the church, and one releasing an ultimate and final revolution. Thereby the revolutionary ground of an original apocalypticism is fully called forth, one invisible and unheard in all established Christianity but actually enacted in the deepest expressions of apocalypticism. In Joachism this revolution is called forth by the very symbol of the third *status* or Age of the Spirit, one wholly transcending the historical ages of the Father and the Son, and a final Age of the Spirit that is truly reborn in the modern world. Here, it is fully reborn in Hegel, that Hegel who could enact the three ages of the Spirit throughout his thinking, and who could declare in the preface to the *Phenomenology of Spirit* that our epoch is the birth time of a new and final Age of the Spirit.

Today Hegel can be known as a genuinely apocalyptic thinker and our only fully apocalyptic philosopher apart from Nietzsche, and it is just thereby that Hegel and Nietzsche are revolutionary thinkers. This is most fully manifest in that death of God which each decisively enacts, a death of God ending or wholly transforming all previous history, for in each the death of God is a full and final apocalyptic event. If only thereby this is a uniquely modern apocalypticism, a modern apocalypticism that is nowhere more distant from ancient apocalypticism than in its enactment of the death of God. Yet we must remember that the prophetic revolution violently assaulted that God which was manifest upon its horizon, or that God which was the established God of an Israelite monarchy and cultus, just as a prophetic iconoclasm shattered all archaic or primordial religion. Primordial religion is deeply grounded in the movement of eternal return, but revolutionary prophets called forth an absolutely new future ending every possibility of eternal return, and a revolutionary future turning the world upside down. At this crucial point Hegel and Nietzsche are in deep continuity with these prophets, and so too is all genuinely modern apocalypticism, so that modern conservative thinkers can know apocalypticism itself as an ultimate threat.

Now we must not confuse a fully modern apocalypticism with that popular apocalypticism that is so fully at hand in our world, and while both are assaults upon every given or established ground of the world, popular apocalypticism is truly a backward movement, whereas a genuinely modern apocalypticism effects a forward movement. An actual forward movement of history, or its envisionment, was only born with the advent of apocalypticism, and a decisive sign of a deeper apocalypticism is its reversal of the primordial movement of eternal return. Thus Nietzsche's vision of eternal recurrence should not be confused with an archaic vision of eternal return, for it is only possible as a consequence of the death of God, or as a consequence of the final ending of every transcendence that is not a purely and totally immanent transcendence. So too both Blake and Hegel can be understood as reversing every possible movement of eternal return, and while this is not true of the early Blake, it is true of the mature Blake, or that Blake who gave us those genuinely apocalyptic epics *Milton* and *Jerusalem.* These are the epics in which Blake most fully enacts the death of God, a death of God that is not only an apocalyptic death, but that can call forth the dead body of God as the very body of Satan. This is that Satan whom Hegel can know as Abstract Spirit or the Bad Infinite, but this is a Satan who is only manifest with the advent of the Age of the Spirit. Apocalypticism inevitably centers upon Satan, or upon an absolute darkness or an absolute evil, but we have been given unique visions of Satan in modern apocalypticism, and unique because they are total visions of Satan, visions calling forth the totality of an absolute darkness.

While this is most clearly true of Blake and Nietzsche, it can be apprehended as occurring throughout our late modern literature and art, just as it occurs in thinkers as diverse as Heidegger and Levinas. If our deepest naming of darkness is an apocalyptic naming, this can only fully occur in the context of an apocalyptic ending, and the apocalyptic ending of darkness itself. Hence a genuinely apocalyptic ending is inseparable from a truly apocalyptic beginning, the beginning of that new creation reversing an old creation, a new creation that is an absolutely new beginning, or an absolutely new world or totality. *Novitas mundi* is a genuinely apocalyptic symbol, and a uniquely apocalyptic symbol insofar as it calls forth a new totality, a new totality that is the consequence of an absolute apocalypse. If Jesus can now be understood as having enacted an absolute apocalypse, and an absolute apocalypse that he named as the Kingdom of God, that apocalyptic kingdom certainly cannot be understood as the eternal reign of God, for it is possible only when every authority and every power of an old creation has come to an end.

Not until Jesus is Satan fully named in the ancient world, and if the great body of the New Testament can know Jesus's deepest conflict as a conflict with Satan, that is a conflict which is reborn in the modern world. For this is nothing less than an apocalyptic conflict or war, a war between absolutely opposing worlds, as manifest not only in modern communism and fascism, but in a uniquely modern war against an absolute evil or an absolute darkness. Historically, apocalypticism is inseparable from an ultimate struggle, and not only against external enemies but even more deeply against enemies within. A Pauline dichotomy between *sarx* and *pneuma* or "flesh" and Spirit is an apocalyptic dichotomy, but here it is a dichotomy wholly within, and within that apocalyptic body of Christ that has not yet undergone a final resurrection. This is that dichotomous body in which a war between "flesh" and Spirit occurs, and this is a war between the "I" of *sarx* and the "I" of *pneuma*, one marking the very advent of a fully dichotomous consciousness.

For this is a consciousness truly divided against itself, a doubled and self-alienated consciousness, a consciousness alone making possible a genuine self-consciousness. If that is the consciousness that becomes the uniquely Western "subject," or a uniquely Western interiority, it is just thereby a self-divided subject, or a subject in ultimate conflict with itself. That too is at bottom an apocalyptic conflict, one impossible apart from an apocalyptic origin, and impossible apart from an apocalyptic dichotomy. Just as such a consciousness is truly absent from the pre-Christian world, it is ever more fully realized in Western consciousness, and its ending only occurs with the uniquely modern realization of the death of God. Both Blake and Nietzsche enacted that ending, an ending that is a uniquely modern apocalyptic ending, but now one embodied in the world as a whole.

Yet there is a genuine continuity between a Pauline apocalypticism and a modern apocalypticism, or between an original Christian apocalypticism and a fully modern apocalypticism, both are grounded in an ultimate and absolute ending and both call forth an absolutely new world. Nowhere is this continuity more fully manifest than in the Christian epic tradition, and nowhere else may one more fully discover an evolution of the uniquely Western subject; just as there is a genuine continuity between Dante, Milton, Blake, and Joyce, this is a reflection of a uniquely Western voyage. If that voyage culminates in Here Comes Everybody, that everybody is a final apocalyptic everybody, and an everybody finally emptied of subject or interiority itself. Clearly this is an apocalyptic condition, but it also can be known as a nihilistic condition, as a consciousness is born that is empty of every ultimate ground. Nietzsche's ultimate war was with nihilism, a nihilism that he could know as a consequence of the death of God; as his madman declares (*The Gay Science* §125), we are straying as through an infinite nothing and can actually feel the breath of empty space.

An apocalyptic willing of the end of the world can be known as a nihilistic willing; it certainly is so insofar as it wills the ending of all and everything, and just as Nietzsche could know Christianity as the origin of our nihilism, and the uniquely Christian God as the deification of nothingness, the will to nothingness pronounced holy (*The Anti-Christ* §18), a pure apocalypticism is the deepest of all assaults upon the world itself. Yet modern apocalypticism has given us our most pathological movements, as in that Nazism which could know itself as the Third Reich or the final Age of the Spirit, a pathology impossible apart from an apocalyptic origin, and impossible apart from an apocalyptic willing of the end of the world. Thus if apocalyptic movements can become mass movements in the late modern world, and mass movements that are the most pathological movements in our history, thereby is unveiled a uniquely modern pathology, and one inseparable from the advent of a mass nihilism.

Just as we are bereft of a common conception of apocalypticism, so likewise are we bereft of a common conception of nihilism, one absent even among our scholars of nihilism, yet we surely know how important or how pervasive both apocalypticism and nihilism are in our world, and how vital it is that we come to grips with them. Is it possible that each of them is integrally related to the other, or that a uniquely modern apocalypticism is inseparable from a uniquely modern nihilism? Dostoevsky's *The Possessed* is that novel which most clearly foresees the advent of a nihilistic apocalypticism, a work that many can understand as the most prophetic novel of the twentieth century and beyond, and a novel that also can be known as our most deeply political novel. It foresees the advent of a mass nihilism, but a mass nihilism that is an apocalyptic nihilism, and an apocalyptic nihilism consuming everything in its wake.

Is it possible that an apocalyptic nihilism is now more powerful than ever before, one embodied in the world as a whole, and yet one wholly disguised to those who most fully embody it? Islamic radicals can now see America itself as such a nihilistic body, an America that is the Great Satan, and a Great Satan who dominates the world. Now if the great American epic is *Moby-Dick*, and *Moby-Dick* too foresees our nihilism, then could Moby Dick or the White Whale be a symbolic image of a new and postmodern nihilism? The very whiteness of Moby Dick is a pure anonymity; here is an absolute nothingness that is the deepest ground of actuality itself, and a nothingness that is an absolute evil or an absolute darkness. Hence it can be understood as an apocalyptic darkness, and a uniquely modern apocalyptic darkness, a darkness that its beholder can see as pure light, or that pure light evoked by the very symbol of whiteness.

Traditional Christian theology has long known that Satan will appear in the last days as an Angel of Light, just as it knows a coming Antichrist who will deceive all the peoples of the earth, for apocalypse itself is a time of absolute reversal, when the world will be turned upside down. Then, wherever power is manifest, or any exterior power, there stands the mark of the Beast, and the greater the power at hand the greater the presence of Satan, for a demonic or a satanic power can then be measured by the very degree of worldly power. Here, the category of "worldly" is all too important, for now worldliness of any kind could only embody a demonic power, and while such imagery is alien to the Hebrew Bible and to all the scriptures in the world until the advent of Christianity, such an understanding of worldliness dominates the New Testament and virtually every subsequent apocalyptic text. Now even if there is no understanding of nihilism itself in our apocalyptic traditions, its full counterpart is manifest here, for not only will the "worldly" ones finally be consumed in an apocalyptic fire, but even now they embody that ultimate yet all too actual nothingness.

In this perspective, we can see that the category of an actual nothingness is born with apocalypticism, or with a full apocalypticism, and just as it is found nowhere outside an apocalyptic horizon, it is reborn in modern apocalypticism, and most purely so in Hegel's *Science of Logic*. Thereafter it ever more fully enters our deeper imaginative enactments, just as it becomes embodied in a late modern consciousness and society; thus Nietzsche and a host of others could know the advent of a new and total nihilism, and one that becomes manifest for all to see in twentieth-century totalitarianism. So even if we have no common conception of nihilism, it would be fatuous to pretend that it does not exist, or that it is not truly powerful in our world. Indeed, it could be disguised in the new world of postmodernity more fully than ever before, and if that world is the most totally technological world in history, and one in which a new and total exteriority is overwhelming all interiority, this can be understood as a nihilistic dissolution of everything that our consciousness and history has embodied. Heidegger understood our new technology in just this way, and such a judgment is now occurring among innumerable critics, just as it is a commonplace in our public domain that a new postmodernity is a new nihilism.

But if it is a new nihilism, it is even thereby a new apocalypticism, an apocalypticism enacting the ending of an old world, and simultaneously enacting the beginning of an absolutely new world. That ending and that beginning are inseparable, and that very inseparability is a genuine sign of a full apocalypticism, one fully manifest in both an ancient and a modern apocalypticism. Now just as we are bereft of an apocalyptic theology, and of a truly critical understanding of apocalypticism itself, we are thereby naked in confronting a new apocalypticism, or in confronting that actual world which is now at hand. How revealing that in response to a major assault, and to the apparent advent of a new world terrorism, virtually no investigation of either apocalypticism or nihilism has occurred; it is as though these are wholly irrelevant to the crisis at hand, despite the apparent apocalyptic and nihilistic identity of the terrorists. While it is possible to identify genuine parallels between Islamic and Christian fundamentalists, their apocalyptic ground is commonly ignored, and thereby their ultimately radical ground is veiled, and veiled if only because we have so little understanding of apocalypticism.

Let us remember that a tiny Jewish apocalyptic sect finally turned the world upside down, and that an originally apocalyptic Islam became one of the greatest powers in world history, and that a uniquely modern apocalypticism became the most revolutionary power in history. Genuine apocalypticism is at bottom revolutionary, and uniquely modern revolutionary movements can all be understood as being apocalyptic, for even the scientific revolution of the seventeenth century can be known as an apocalyptic revolution insofar as it could only give birth to an absolutely new world by bringing an old world to an end. If the advent of Christianity was a revolutionary event, its ultimate revolution is inseparable from its original apocalyptic core, and that Christianity which is least revolutionary today, or least threatening to anyone, is a wholly non-apocalyptic Christianity. So likewise with Marxism, once its original apocalyptic ground had become abated, Marxism ceased to be revolutionary and soon collapsed altogether. Commonly apocalypticism is known as the sheerest fantasy, or as the most backward of all possible movements, but historically genuine apocalypticism has been the very opposite, and it has had no rival as an ultimately revolutionary power.

Yes, we should understand genuine apocalypticism as being genuinely revolutionary, and this in both its ancient and its modern expressions. At no point is there greater continuity between modern and ancient apocalypticism than at this crucial point, and if a genuine revolution turns the world upside down, it is apocalypticism above all that most fully embodies such a goal. Indeed, the very goal of an absolute world reversal was born with the advent of apocalypticism; thereafter it has inevitably been renewed in modern revolutionary movements, which thereby give witness to their profound debt to ancient apocalypticism. All the great political revolutions in the modern world have been apocalyptic revolutions, and these begin with the English Revolution, which was our most apocalyptic revolution until the French Revolution, and just as Hegel and virtually every other major thinker of his time could know the French Revolution as the great dividing line in world history, the French Revolution truly brought a world to an end. But so likewise did the Russian and the Chinese revolutions, and even if these have now reversed or abated themselves, each had an enormous impact upon world history, and nothing has more transformed the world than our modern revolutions.

Now we seemingly stand at the very end of this revolutionary history, and if a new and comprehensive conservatism now dominates the world, that conservatism is inseparable from a new technological world, or from a new and total exteriority, and one profoundly transforming both consciousness and society. That very transformation could be understood as an apocalyptic transformation, surely so if an old world is now being brought to an end, and certainly so if an absolutely new world is now at hand. So that if our revolutionary history is now ending, that very ending could be the inauguration of a new and even more total revolution, and perhaps a revolution transforming our history as has none previously. If a new apocalypse is now being born, and a truly revolutionary apocalypse, is that a wholly negative apocalypse, or could it be an apocalypse that is absolutely negative and absolutely positive at once?

The truth is that every apocalypse we have known is truly positive and negative simultaneously; already this is true of the prophetic revolution, a revolution inseparable from the ending of an ancient Israel, thereby being inseparable from the catastrophe of the exile of Israel, an exile in which Israel lost every ground of an ancient people. So too an original Christian apocalypse effected an absolute ending, an ending not only of what now can be known as an "old" covenant and an "old" Israel, but the ending of that historical world that existed before Christ. No greater historical transformation had occurred in the world, and this is truly a negative transformation insofar as it ended the Classical world, ultimately issuing in what even the Christian knows as the Dark Ages. Thus Nietzsche could know the advent of Christianity as the most catastrophic event that has ever occurred. And if there truly is a uniquely modern apocalypse, that apocalypse is positive and negative simultaneously, a negativity fully manifest in what we are now undergoing as the end of Western history.

Once again let us recall the ultimate difference between the backward movement of a primordial eternal return and the forward movement of full or genuine apocalypticism; each can be understood as the very opposite of the other, and each is far more powerful than we commonly realize. A primordial religion of eternal return can be understood as having been religion itself for hundreds of thousands of years, and in one form or another it is found in all our major religions, even including Judaism, Christianity, and Islam. Only the prophetic traditions within our monotheistic religions have truly challenged an eternal return, and this challenge has occurred again and again, for eternal return has not only returned again and again in these religions, but it is inseparable from their most powerful orthodoxies. This is most true in Christianity itself, which was the first tradition in a non-Oriental world to call forth an absolutely primordial Godhead, and the way to that Godhead is the way of eternal return. Indeed, the very advent of that Godhead can be understood as a profound reaction against a Christian apocalypticism, one reversing the forward movement of that apocalypticism into the backward movement of eternal return. Thence primordial Godhead becomes all in all in Christianity, and apocalyptic Godhead becomes invisible or wholly subterranean, but even if an apocalyptic Godhead has been subterranean and invisible, it has nevertheless been overwhelmingly powerful in a uniquely Western apocalypticism.

A decisive sign of that apocalypticism was the advent of an overwhelming sense of the forward movement of history in early modernity;

this had never before predominated in the world, or not apart from apocalyptic movements, and it marks an ultimate dividing line between the modern world and every ancient world. Accompanying this truly new consciousness and sensibility is a realization of the actual and final pastness of the past, as for the first time there is a realization that we can never return to the past, can never recover a past moment of either time or history. This was a truly revolutionary realization, not only making actually impossible every backward movement, but above all ending every possibility of eternal return. But has this deeply and uniquely modern realization come to an end, are we now losing every sense of the actual possibility of a truly forward movement, and does this bring with it a renewal of eternal return?

It is fascinating that the return of philosophy to theology that has occurred in postmodernity is a return not only to a deeply conservative theology, as in Levinas and Derrida and their innumerable followers, but also a renewal of the primordial movement of eternal return. Is it possible that our new technological world has occasioned such a return, a world ending everything that we have known as interiority and thus making possible a return to a pre-interior or pre-self-conscious world? If it is selfhood itself, or a truly individual selfhood that is now ending, is that an ending inseparable from a renewal of eternal return? Certainly the primordial world of eternal return is a pre-interior world, and the deepest expressions of eternal return in all post-primordial worlds are dissolutions or transfigurations of all interiority. If late modernity or postmodernity is embodying a renewal of eternal return, is that a renewal inseparable from a dissolution of everything that the West has known as subject or self-consciousness? If so, could this finally be a forward rather than a backward movement, thus at bottom an apocalyptic rather than a primordial movement?

Just as it was an early Christian apocalypticism that generated a new interiority, a truly dichotomous interiority polarized by the apocalyptic opposites of "flesh" and Spirit, and a doubled or self-divided interiority in profound conflict with itself, is the ending of every such interiority simply and only a dissolution of interiority? Or could it be a truly comprehensive realization of that self-negation which inaugurates this interiority, a self-negation deeply negating itself, and a self-negation inseparable from what we have known as interiority and self-consciousness? Our fullest apocalyptic philosophy, the dialectical philosophy of Hegel, is a philosophy not simply grounded in an absolute self-negation but a philosophy realizing self-negation or self-emptying in every domain whatsoever. No philosophy has ever been a more absolute or total philosophy, yet this is a philosophy of absolute self-negation, and perhaps no other feature could more fully unveil its genuine apocalyptic identity, even its genuinely Christian apocalyptic identity. Just as Hegel could profoundly understand the Crucifixion as the self-negation of the Godhead, thereby inaugurating a conceptual realization of the death of God, he understood that self-negation as passing into historical actuality itself, thereby realizing the third and final Age of the Spirit.

Could that ending of interiority into which we are being initiated be yet a further actualization of that final age, whereby it would be not only an apocalyptic ending but even thereby an apocalyptic beginning, and an absolute beginning of an absolute apocalypse? Of course, the Christian knows this beginning as having originally occurred in Christ, but that beginning has not only been continually transformed in our history, it has also continually been renewed, renewals that are not only transforming renewals but ever more comprehensive renewals of that original beginning. While these have proceeded in both positive and negative directions, and have often seemingly reversed that original beginning, such reversals are inseparable from their very opposites, opposites themselves issuing in renewals of apocalypticism, and above all so in our most revolutionary movements. How ironic that it was the ending of Christendom that called forth our most radical and comprehensive apocalyptic movements, for not even Joachism is as comprehensive an apocalypticism as are our fully modern apocalypticisms, nor was Joachism as openly revolutionary.

Now just as the advent of a new and total darkness is a decisive apocalyptic sign, it is not possible actually to name or envision that darkness apart from a genuinely apocalyptic horizon, so that a full naming or a full envisionment of a truly new and total darkness is the consequence of a new apocalyptic horizon. Is such naming or such envisionment occurring in our world? This would certainly appear to have occurred in our late modern literature and art, but is it occurring in the new world of postmodernity, or in the full actuality of our world? Surely a new and ultimate silence prevails among us, a silence precluding that deeper naming or that deeper envisionment which we once knew. Is that silence itself an apocalyptic sign, and one seemingly the very opposite of all previous apocalyptic conditions? As Kafka and

Wittgenstein taught us so deeply, there is no greater virtue than a genuine silence, nor a more difficult one, but is our new silence a genuine silence or a simple speechlessness? Yes, our new silence is seemingly inseparable from a new ubiquity of idle and meaningless speech, the most vacuous and empty language in our history, and so empty as apparently to be free of that self-alienation and self-laceration which once accompanied an empty language, as though no selfhood now remains that could undergo self-alienation at all.

Could this condition itself be necessary and essential for a new apocalypse? Just as the prophetic tradition of Israel could know that a new apocalypse is inseparable from a new and absolute judgment, could such a judgment be occurring today, and occurring as those ancient prophets proclaimed throughout our consciousness and society? Paul knew apocalyptic judgment as a universal judgment, not only comprehending the world itself, but calling forth every manifest or given world as an "old" world, and one even now coming to an end. Yet for the early Christian this apocalyptic condition was the occasion for an ecstatic joy, for it is inseparable from the full and final advent of the Kingdom of God, as an absolutely new Jerusalem is now being born. Is a new Jerusalem present upon our horizon, or its very opposite? Is it only a backward moving apocalypticism that can now know a new Jerusalem, a new Jerusalem that the full actuality of our consciousness could only know as an iron cage? It was Weber who gave us the image of a uniquely modern iron cage, just as it was Weber who first discovered the apocalyptic ground of the prophetic movement of Israel, and while Weber ended his life in despair, he gave us our fullest understanding of a uniquely modern secularization, one inseparable from its prophetic and apocalyptic ground. Is that secularization now realizing its final consummation, and are we now being stripped of every genuinely religious ground, even while being overwhelmed by an empty and destructive religiosity?

Yes, when God is dead religion is everywhere, and everywhere as a vacuous and destructive power, but this is just the judgment that ancient apocalypticism reached in reaction against all the established religion upon its horizon, knowing that religion as the Great Beast or the Great Whore. So, too, our modern apocalyptic prophets have assaulted the religion upon their horizon, and if assaults upon religion have become rare in our new world, is that a sign that ours is a non-apocalyptic condition? Or is this yet another sign of our new silence, and perhaps even an apocalyptic silence, a silence that our greatest New Testament theologian, Bultmann, could know as occurring in Jesus. But if this is a pure silence it is inseparable from the purest speech or the purest Word. Is any such Word present upon our horizon, and if so, can we hear it only as a genuine silence, and a silence inseparable from a genuine transfiguration or a genuine apocalypse? Yes, apocalypse for us could only be a new apocalypse, an absolutely new apocalypse, and perhaps even thereby invisible and unheard as apocalypse itself.

—NOVEMBER 2002

3

RENEWING THE KINGDOM OF GOD

Both Hegel and Nietzsche are great masters of historical irony, and just as each reached deeply ironical understandings of the history of Christianity, understandings that strangely parallel even if they invert each other, each could understand that history as an absolute history, and an absolute history culminating in apocalypse. For Hegel, the history of Christianity is the history of the absolute religion, but an absolute religion of absolute self-negation, a self-negation nevertheless realizing an absolute power, and an absolute power finally realizing itself as the totality of history, and this occurs precisely when history itself comes to an end. Nietzsche's understanding of Christianity is seemingly the opposite of this, for the history of Christianity is the history of an absolute nihilism or absolute No-saying, and it only comes to an end with the death of the Christian God, but that is an apocalyptic death issuing in the advent of a new Zarathustra or a new absolute Yes-saying. In *The Anti-Christ*, Nietzsche understands Christianity as becoming the very opposite of Jesus, hence its gospel is a *dysangel*, and is the origin of our deepest *ressentiment*. Hegel, too, believed that Christianity is only possible with the dissolution or ending of Jesus, but that ending makes possible the advent of a totally new world and horizon, one that is an absolute historical power, and one inaugurated by the crucifixion of Jesus. That crucifixion is only fully historically actualized with the modern realization of the death of God, and it is the death of the uniquely Christian God that for both Hegel and Nietzsche is the actualization of an absolutely new world, a new world that is absolute apocalypse.

31

Certainly Hegel and Nietzsche both give us deeply important even if profoundly ironical understandings of the Kingdom of God, a kingdom that seemingly reverses itself, but that is the very reversal realizing its greatest power, or its greatest historical power, and this is so even in its purely negative expressions; while Nietzsche and Hegel have discrepant if not opposite understandings of the negative, it is the negative itself that is of overwhelming importance for each of them, a pure negativity inseparable from the realization of the Kingdom of God. Hegel and Nietzsche are our only philosophers who ultimately engage Jesus and who are truly open to his language and praxis, and nowhere in contemporary theology do we encounter such an ultimate and profound engagement. Just as Nietzsche effects a profound renewal even if reversal of the language and praxis of Jesus in *Thus Spoke Zarathustra*, Hegel conceptually recreates the absolutely kenotic way of Jesus into the absolute self-negation of the *Phenomenology of Spirit* and the absolute self-emptying of the *Science of Logic*.

What an ultimate irony it is to compare such an understanding of the Kingdom of God with those we encounter in theology and New Testament scholarship today; how profound is the one and how shallow the other, and how closed are contemporary New Testament scholarship and theology to any deeper understanding of Jesus! But this was not true only a generation or two ago, and above all not in a pre-Nazi Germany. Then the worlds of theology and biblical scholarship were as enlightened as any other, and a Bultmann and a Heidegger could engage in genuine dialogue and cooperation. German philosophers were often not only theologically enlightened but theologically sophisticated, and just as such sophistication is unknown today, theology has virtually come to an end in our academic world, while biblical scholarship exists only in its peripheries. But is this an opportunity for a genuinely radical theology, one truly engaged with the language and praxis of Jesus, and would such an engagement necessarily be radical and ultimately against the grain? Perhaps ours is the first world in which simply to think theologically is to engage in a radical venture; surely our religious worlds are more closed to genuine theology than ever previously, yet religion is seemingly more powerful today than it has been since the advent of modernity, and never before in our history has it been so immune to or so removed from all possibility of ultimate challenge.

Nothing has been more fully demonstrated in modern biblical criticism and scholarship than the primacy of the Kingdom of God in the proclamation, parables, and praxis of Jesus, but at no other point is our New Testament criticism and theology more alienated from a new testament or new covenant, or more bound to an old covenant and old aeon. This is manifest in the almost universal tendency to interpret this Kingdom as a monarchic "rule" or "reign," thereby understanding it through ancient imperial categories that already were under assault in the prophetic revolution, and that are at the furthest possible remove from the actual language and acts of Jesus. Despite the enormous skepticism that has developed about our knowledge of the language of Jesus, there are few scholars who doubt that "Kingdom of God" is primary in that language, just as it is also true that as far as we can know "Kingdom of God" does not enter writing itself until the New Testament, not even in the Dead Sea Scrolls where we might most expect it.

It is difficult to resist the judgment that "Kingdom of God" is an eschatological or apocalyptic title, and if so it could only mean "kingdom" or "reign" in a sense wholly other than all given or ancient meanings of "kingdom" or "reign," including all those meanings that have entered our theologies. At no other point have our theologies been more profoundly alienated both from Jesus and the New Testament, thereby bringing modern theology to an ultimate crisis, and while that crisis is now pervasively hidden and disguised, it is openly reenacted with every critical attempt to discover or recover a New Testament theology.

Perhaps it is the parables of Jesus that most openly embody this crisis, for while it is clear that all the parables are parables of the Kingdom of God, traditionally these have for the most part been understood as allegories of an eternal Heaven, allegories at a virtually infinite distance from the language of the Bible, hence such allegorical interpretations come to an end in modern New Testament scholarship. One motif is clear in most of the parables, and that is not simply an assault upon but a reversal of all given hierarchies or values, as the world itself is turned upside down. So, too, a given or manifest God here disappears, as does all biblical or revelatory language, and while an ultimate enactment does indeed occur, it occurs in absolutely ordinary language and ordinary events. Mystery here comes to an end, even the deepest mystery, and if this occurs in a truly new language, this is a language that has never since been repeated, as the great body of Christianity evolved into new language worlds as far as possible removed from this beginning.

Now if the common understanding of Kingdom of God as the "rule" or "reign" of God truly reverses the kingdom that Jesus enacted, and if this is true of every sovereign or monarchic image, then not only is a radical iconoclasm present in the praxis of Jesus, but an actual dissolution of the manifest or the given God. Jesus may well have been responsible for a far deeper blasphemy than any that is recorded in the gospels, just as he may have created a far greater offense than any that we can imagine, and done so in his very enactment of the Kingdom of God, an enactment that is a disenactment of every other ultimate ground, and therefore a disenactment of "God." Jesus, of course, is in deep continuity with the prophetic tradition, and the prophetic revolution disenacted every previous epiphany of God, but did so by an open assault upon the established or the given God, whereas Jesus effects a "silent" dissolution of that God, and one that may be all the more powerful because of its silence. A truly new iconoclasm is present in Jesus, even an invisible or silent iconoclasm, one the consequence of the advent of an absolutely new immediacy of God, an immediacy of God that is the Kingdom of God, but an immediacy that is lost or reversed with every pronunciation of the name of God, or every evocation of God as God. Both Paul and the Fourth Gospel renew and reenact this iconoclasm, but they do so with truly new evocations of God as God, whereas the parabolic Jesus of the synoptic gospels gives us a pure iconoclasm with no enactment of God as God.

This is surely a fundamental reason why the Kingdom of God is such a mystery for us, as the enactment and praxis of Jesus is not an enactment of "God" but far rather an enactment of that Kingdom of God that is a kenotic kingdom, or an enactment of the self-emptying or the self-negation of God as God, and only thereby an enactment of an absolutely new apocalypse of God. Nothing less than an absolutely new apocalypse of God could make possible the actual advent of a new aeon or new creation, and if Kingdom of God is an absolutely new "kingdom," it could only be wholly other than a monarchic "kingdom," and thus wholly other than an imperial "reign" of God. Thus to know God as absolute Lord and only absolute Lord is to refuse God as Suffering Servant and Crucified God; this refusal is just the path of Christian orthodoxy, an orthodoxy refusing the death of God in the crucifixion, thereby refusing not only the kenotic God but a kenotic redemption, hence knowing redemption not only as exaltation but as a heavenly deification or spiritualization. Nothing could be further from the absolutely new life enacted by the eschatological and parabolic Jesus, for it is Christian "spirituality" that most betrays that life, betraying it not only in its otherworldliness, but in its refusal of absolute *novum* itself, a refusal that is inevitable for any way that is archaic or primordial, and likewise for any way that is disincarnate or otherworldly.

Not only is the name of God unspoken in the parables, but a language is enacted that cannot speak that name, and cannot speak it if only because of the pure immediacy here called forth, an immediacy alien to every possible absolute transcendence. While the name of God is continually evoked in the gospels, this does not occur in the parables, and if the parables are truly free of allegory, and even free of everything commonly manifest as metaphor, then it is highly doubtful that there is an opening to anything we know as God in the parabolic language of Jesus, and yet Jesus taught primarily by way of parabolic enactment. Could it be that Jesus enacted a way that is free of everything we know as God, of everything we know as transcendence itself? And could this occur precisely in his enactment of the Kingdom of God, a kingdom whose absolute immediacy is wholly other than "God"?

Have we today been given a truly new realization of the Kingdom of God, one that is all in all but never manifest as itself? Even as Jesus is an ultimate icon in our world, is that Kingdom of God that he enacted and proclaimed truly at hand in the brute actuality of our world? Early Christians could know the Kingdom of God as being actually at hand in their world, a world as violent as, if not more violent, than any other, and a world truly embodying an ultimate darkness and abyss, but it is in that abysmal desert that the Kingdom of God realizes itself, and even if this occurs as a total judgment, it also occurs as a total transfiguration, and one immediately at hand in the Parousia itself. Yet it was the delay of the Parousia that issued in a radical and comprehensive transformation of Christianity, one without parallel in the history of religions, and nothing is more profoundly altered in this transformation than is the Kingdom of God, as it ceased to be an absolutely new totality and became to the contrary an absolutely old totality, or that totality that is the absolute authority and the absolute power of the primordial Creator. Nowhere else in history does such an ultimate and absolute transformation occur, and if the Christian God is unique in its absolute sovereignty and absolute transcendence, the epiphany or realization of that very transcendence and sovereignty can be understood as a consequence of a pure and total reversal of an absolutely immanent and kenotic Kingdom of God.

Indeed, nothing else makes Christianity so unique as does this reversal, one fully paralleled in the transformation of the kenotic Jesus into absolute Lord and Cosmocrator, so much so that Christianity has yet to evolve a truly or purely kenotic christology, and kenotic images of Jesus inevitably appear as ultimate challenges to all established or all given Christianity. Now it is truly ironic that virtually all theologians understand the Kingdom of God as the "rule" or "reign" of God, thereby sanctioning the greatest of all historical transformations, and doing so as though they were simply being loyal to the New Testament, whereas they are far rather being loyal to the authority of the established church. That even critical New Testament scholars can embody such loyalty is truly remarkable, and while this never occurs in our major philosophical investigations of the New Testament (e.g., those of Hegel, Nietzsche, Heidegger), the latter are wholly repressed in our theological worlds and hidden in the world at large. Why such a deep fear of critical thinking about the New Testament? Is Jesus himself far more revolutionary than we can imagine, and perhaps most revolutionary in his enactment of the Kingdom of God, a kingdom that must be purely reversed to make possible everything we know as world, and everything that is manifest to us as life itself?

Certainly there is no possibility of apprehending the Kingdom of God that Jesus enacted if we do so through our established categories of authority and power, and if this is just what occurs in our theology and New Testament scholarship today, can the contemporary interpretation of Kingdom of God as "divine sovereignty" be understood as a pure reversal of the Kingdom of God so as to realize an absolutely primordial Creator and Lord? Thereby the absolutely new is reversed into the absolutely primordial, but such a reversal is only possible as a consequence of the advent of the absolutely new. Indeed, ways of eternal return are alien to the West until the advent of Christianity, and one of the most consequential innovations of ancient Christianity was not only the inauguration in a post-archaic world of a way of eternal return, but an epiphany or realization of Godhead itself as an absolutely primordial Godhead. Cannot this very inauguration, an ultimate inauguration, be understood as only being possible through a pure and total reversal of the absolutely new, an absolutely new which is that Kingdom of God that Jesus enacted and proclaimed?

When Godhead is deeply and ultimately apprehended as primordial Godhead, the only way to that Godhead is the way of *return*, finally the way of eternal return, one that was ever more fully realized in ancient Christianity and that ever more fully distanced itself from every possible eschatological way, every possible eschatological ground, including that eschatological ground that had been the original ground of Christianity. This was a primary source of the genesis of Christian heresy, including the deepest Christian heresy. Just as the orthodox God is an ever more fully primordial God, the heretical Christian God is an ever more fully eschatological God, or is so in the most powerful and decisive Christian heresies. This is above all true in the modern world, as fully exemplified by a Blake or Hegel, so that it is our deepest apocalypticism that is our deepest heresy, and this is true not only in the Christian world but in the parallel worlds of Judaism and Islam, for in all three of these worlds orthodoxy itself came into existence by way of a negation and reversal of apocalypticism. That reversal gave birth to everything that we most deeply know as God, or everything that is most deeply given or manifest to us as God, and inevitably our most radical thinking and vision challenges this God and itself becomes ever more radical as it evolves, a radicality culminating with profound and comprehensive enactments of the death of God.

Yet these enactments can be understood as being in genuine continuity with the eschatological or apocalyptic Jesus, and with the eschatological proclamation and enactment of that Jesus, an enactment of that Kingdom of God which is the absolutely new. Only the pure and total reversal of this Kingdom made possible the advent of the absolutely primordial God, an absolutely primordial God who perishes or dies or is wholly transfigured with the renewal of the absolutely new. Initially, this death is most purely enacted by Blake and Hegel as apocalyptic enactors of an absolutely new apocalypse, and this absolutely new apocalypse is a profound renewal of the eschatological Jesus, thus a renewal of that Kingdom of God that Jesus enacted and proclaimed. Nowhere does such a renewal occur in Christian theology, or in the dominant expressions of that theology, but this is a theology that is a deeply non-apocalyptic or non-eschatological theology, a theology centered upon the absolutely primordial Creator, and therefore centered upon an absolutely sovereign and absolutely transcendent Godhead.

This is the very Godhead whose self-negation or self-emptying is profoundly enacted in both a uniquely modern imagination and a uniquely modern philosophy, as here our deeper philosophical and imaginative enactments are truly coordinate with each other if not united. But can this uniquely modern enactment, the death of God, be understood as a genuine negation and reversal of that uniquely primordial Godhead realized by a reversal of Jesus's Kingdom of God?

From an eschatological or apocalyptic perspective, primordial Godhead could only be an alien Godhead, and from this perspective primordial Godhead and apocalyptic Godhead are genuine opposites, thereby realizing that ultimate conflict that occurs between them in early Christianity, an early Christianity giving birth to Gnosticism, a Gnosticism that is the initial realization of a purely primordial Godhead. A profound conflict between Gnosticism and apocalypticism is at the very center of Paul's genuine letters, and most clearly so in the Corinthian correspondence, but this is a conflict that is reborn in full or late modernity, and reborn in a uniquely modern conflict between primordial and eschatological horizons, as manifest not only in Nietzsche and Heidegger, but throughout a uniquely modern imagination, as witness Milton, Blake, Joyce. For this ultimate conflict between apocalyptic and primordial domains is most comprehensive and most profound in our uniquely modern epic enactments, the seeds of which are fully established by *Paradise Lost*, but which is only fully realized in Blake's *Jerusalem* and Joyce's *Finnegans Wake*. Here an ultimate *coincidentia oppositorum* occurs, and occurs in that absolute apocalypse effecting a final and dialectical union between that Satan who is the absolutely alien God and that Christ who is the apocalyptic Jerusalem, and between a truly primordial Here Comes Everybody and a truly apocalyptic Anna Livia Plurabelle, a dialectical union absolutely transfiguring each of these ultimate opposites, thus absolutely transfiguring every possible apocalyptic or primordial totality. This is perhaps our most ultimate vision of the Kingdom of God.

If so it is a vision in which every given meaning and identity of both the primordial and the apocalyptic truly disappears, a disappearance that perhaps occurs in Nietzsche, and Heidegger too, and a disappearance that can be understood as having first been enacted by the eschatological and parabolic Jesus. This is a disappearance profoundly deepening the mystery of the way of Jesus, for then it can appear neither as an apocalyptic nor a primordial way, or certainly not as a purely apocalyptic or purely primordial way, and if this is a genuine shattering of both apocalyptic and primordial horizons, it nonetheless is an enactment of the full depths of those horizons, which perhaps can be enacted only with this disappearance. So, too, the ethical dimension of this way then becomes even more elusive, unless it is possible that the ethical command or the ethical gift of Jesus is apocalyptic and primordial simultaneously, hence an absolutely new gift that is nonetheless given in the absolutely primordial itself, and a primordial that is only truly itself when it is absolutely new.

Such a vision or epiphany is surely a negation and transcendence of that absolutely primordial Godhead which Christianity has known, but it could be a Hegelian or forward-moving negation, hence one preserving the absolutely primordial itself, but preserving it only by negating it, and negating it absolutely. Only a truly absolute negation could effect a genuine transfiguration of primordial Godhead, a transfiguration issuing in that absolutely primordial that *is* the absolutely new, or that absolutely primordial that is nowhere but here and now. Then all distinction or difference between the primordial and the apocalyptic would have vanished, just as it seemingly does in the parables of Jesus; but then the Kingdom of God enacted by the parables would not only be apocalyptic and primordial at once, but primordial only insofar as it is apocalyptic, and apocalyptic only insofar as it is primordial. Then the absolutely given would be the absolutely new, and the absolutely new would not only be everywhere, but everyone, yet an everyone who is no one, or no one who stands apart from the absolute grace or the absolute gift of the absolutely new. This would be a genuine "ending of the world," and thereby the advent of a truly new life and praxis, an advent that is the advent of the Kingdom of God, yes, but only insofar as such an advent is an absolute ending.

Certainly the advent of the Kingdom of God embodies an absolute ending, but nothing has been more elusive than such an ending, and while it has realized multiple and even contradictory meanings throughout our history, these occur not only over vastly different arenas or fields, but occur as an ultimate mystery, for the mystery of absolute ending or omega is just as deep as the mystery of absolute beginning or genesis. Now if we can be confident that Jesus enacted such an ending, and did so in his enactment of the Kingdom of God, that ending is nevertheless an absolute beginning, and an absolute beginning occurring here and now. Indeed, such an occurrence is impossible apart from absolute ending, an absolutely actual ending whose actuality is inseparable from the actuality of absolute beginning, and inseparable from the actuality of that absolute beginning occurring even now. That occurrence is the advent of the Kingdom of God, an advent that is absolute ending and beginning at once, and is absolute ending only insofar as it is absolute beginning, so that ending is an absolute grace or absolute gift, and the sole source of blessedness itself.

—JULY 2005

4

HEGEL

The *Phenomenology of Spirit* as Ground
of a Uniquely Modern Theology

The past generation has witnessed a discovery of the deeply theological ground of modern philosophy, one initiated by Hegel's *Phenomenology of Spirit*, a work that not only revolutionized philosophy
but for the first time created a philosophical realization of the death
of God, a realization that is not only the consummation of Western
philosophy but is the recovery of a long hidden or forgotten ultimate
ground of Christianity itself. This revolutionary theological thinking
is also thereby the advent of a purely apocalyptic philosophical thinking, one reflecting the advent of the final Age of the Spirit, an advent
inseparable from the absolute self-negation or self-emptying of Absolute Spirit. Absolute Spirit is the Hegelian name of the Kingdom of
God, and Kingdom of God is a title or category absent from all traditions and all writing prior to the New Testament, where it is at the
very center of the proclamation and praxis of Jesus, one enacting the
Kingdom of God as dawning here and now, thereby transfiguring absolutely everything whatsoever. Almost immediately Hellenistic Christianity transformed Kingdom of God into the "rule" or "reign" of God,
thereby wholly reversing the original apocalyptic ground of Christianity, the most total transformation of a new way or new world that has
ever occurred in history. Whereas Jesus had enacted and embodied an

absolutely new world, Hellenistic Christianity embodied and enacted the absolute transcendence and absolute sovereignty of God, and thereby it initiated an eternal return to an absolutely primordial Godhead, one that is the very opposite of that Kingdom of God which is dawning here and now, and dawning as that absolute immanence which is an absolute transfiguration.

Hegel effected a philosophical revolution by creating a truly new philosophical method, a method that is an absolute self-negation or self-emptying, and one that can be understood as a philosophical appropriation of the kenotic or uniquely self-emptying way of Jesus, one to which theology has been closed except for the very beginning of our theology in Paul. The uniquely Pauline word "kenosis" appears at some of the most decisive points of the *Phenomenology*, and just as Hegel is a truly Pauline thinker, this most fundamentally occurs in his apprehension and enactment of the death of God, a purely conceptual enactment of absolute death that is the first conceptual enactment of the Crucifixion, and just as the Crucifixion is at the center of Paul's theology, the death of God is at the center of Hegel's philosophy. This is the center making possible the first full philosophical enactment of an absolute immanence, an absolute immanence that is the total self-negation or self-emptying of an absolute transcendence, and only an apprehension of that immanence makes possible an understanding of a total self-emptying or self-negation, for the Hegelian philosophical revolution is inseparable from the uniquely modern historical realization of a final and ultimate death of God.

Not only is the Hegelian revolution the first purely philosophical apocalyptic thinking, but it is also and even thereby the first purely philosophical historical thinking, not only creating the philosophy of history, but recreating philosophy itself as a profoundly historical thinking. This thinking is born in the *Phenomenology of Spirit*, as the ultimate events of our history now pass into philosophical thinking itself, and pure thinking for the first time becomes a truly historical thinking. Yet this is a historical thinking that is simultaneously an apocalyptic thinking, a historical thinking released by the advent of the final Age of the Spirit, one concretely occurring in the French Revolution, and for Hegel the French Revolution is a world-historical event, one inaugurating the last stage of history and issuing in a new world in which secular life or history is the incarnate embodiment of Absolute Spirit or the Kingdom of God. Now an ecstatic joy is released in the world, and an actual dawning occurs of a new and absolute freedom, and if this is a universal freedom it is initially a cold and abstract one, an abstract universality destroying all historical traditions and reducing the individual to a bare integer of existence. The sole act and deed of this wholly abstract individual is therefore death, a new death that has no inner significance whatsoever, or no more significance than swallowing a mouthful of water, for this universal freedom is actually the fury of destruction, one embodied in the terror of the French Revolution.

Now the French Revolution is the historical point at which a universal consciousness first becomes fully actual and real; it is so most clearly and decisively in the antithesis that now arises between universal freedom and the individuality of an actual self-consciousness, an antithesis that is the source of a new universal energy and will. For the full advent of an abstract and objective consciousness is inseparable from the birth of a new interior and subjective consciousness, an "I" or self-consciousness that is purely and only itself, and is only itself by virtue of an objective and universal consciousness that is the intrinsic and necessary other of itself. The very interior depths of this new subjective consciousness are inseparable from their ground in the universality and totality of a new objective consciousness, for a universal consciousness can actually realize itself objectively only by absolutely negating its own subjective ground or pole. While death is now and for the first time objectively meaningless and insignificant, it is subjectively more real than ever before, and thus death becomes the one and only portal to a full and final subjective and interior resolution and fulfillment. Hegel's term for that form of consciousness that realizes itself by losing all the essence and substance of itself is the Unhappy Consciousness, a consciousness that realizes itself by realizing that *God himself is dead* (*Phenomenology* 785).

But this hard saying is the expression of innermost self-knowledge, the return of consciousness into the depths of the night in which "I" *is* "I," a night no longer distinguishing or knowing anything outside of itself. Yes, this is an ultimate and total loss of substance, but it is simultaneously the pure subjectivity of substance or the pure certainty of itself that it lacked when it was object or pure essence. Consequently, this is the inbreathing of the Spirit whereby Substance becomes Subject, by which all abstraction and lifelessness have died, and Substance has become an actual and universal Self-Consciousness. Nowhere else does Hegel gives us such a decisive portrait of apocalypse, an apocalypse realized only by the death of God, or only by that Crucifixion which *is* absolute apocalypse, a crucifixion never previously purely thought, just as apocalypse had never been purely thought before, and this can occur only by way of an ultimate revolution in thinking itself.

J. N. Findlay remarks in his book on Hegel that Hegel is alone among philosophers in his purely philosophical realization of the depths of Christian dogma, realizing Creation, Covenant, Incarnation, Crucifixion, Resurrection, and Apocalypse in a new and revolutionary philosophical thinking, when for the first time theology and philosophy wholly coincide or are fully united. Both our philosophical and our theological worlds ignore this extremely important truth, and this alone could account for their mutual alienation from Hegel, an alienation now extending to those profoundly Hegelian thinkers, Kierkegaard and Marx, for even if they are wholly reverse or inverted Hegelian thinkers, their revolutionary impact is inseparable from the inversion or reversal of Hegelian thinking.

So it is that philosophical and theological thinking coincide in Hegel as they had never done before; only Spinoza here anticipates Hegel, aside from perhaps the pre-Socratics, pre-Socratics whom Hegel would resurrect, just as Heidegger has done in the twentieth century. Now in this perspective we must abandon all our given or established understanding of theology; so far from being any form of ecclesiastical or dogmatic theology, here theology is pure thinking itself, a thinking that can only think God or the Godhead by thinking the self-negation or the self-emptying of God, and if Hegel's thinking is truly a purely kenotic thinking, it is so most purely in thinking the absolute self-emptying of Godhead itself. Perhaps what is most remarkable or most startling about this thinking is its recovery of the Kingdom of God, one that had been wholly lost in Christian theology and all too significantly only recovered after the historical realization of the death of God, a death of God dissolving everything that we have known as God, which perhaps alone makes possible a recovery of that Kingdom of God which Jesus enacts and proclaims; one occurring not only in the pure thinking of Hegel but in the revolutionary imaginative vision of William Blake.

Just as Blake has given us our most alien or most negative images of God, wherein God becomes manifest even as Satan, so too Hegel gives us our most negative concepts of God, wherein God not only becomes the Bad Infinite in the *Science of Logic*, but purely abstract

Spirit in the *Phenomenology*, a Spirit that can only be apprehended in a purely negative or empty mode of consciousness, an abstract Spirit that is the inevitable consequence of the evolution of Spirit itself. Nothing is more unique in Hegel than the absolutely forward movement of his thinking, a forward movement that is the evolution of Spirit, but an evolution occurring only through self-negation or self-emptying, and a self-emptying and self-negation wherein everything passes into its own contrary; it is this absolutely contradictory or self-negating movement that is the sole source of all movement and life. Indeed, Hegel has given us our only truly Western dialectical logic, one realizing ultimately revolutionary expressions in both Marx and Kierkegaard, and if no thinkers have been so truly opposite of each other as are Kierkegaard and Marx, such absolute opposition is made possible only by a purely dialectical thinking, one finally promising a *coincidentia oppositorum*.

An ultimate topic that has been abandoned by all given or manifest theological thinking today is redemption itself, above all an absolute redemption, one that is the very center of Hegel's thinking, as is most manifest in the final sections of the *Phenomenology of Spirit*. While the *Phenomenology* can be taken to be the most complex and difficult of all philosophical works, it is possible to understand that a necessary and inevitable evolution of thinking occurs here, one reflecting an evolution of Spirit itself, an evolution in which Spirit realizes itself only by negating or emptying itself. Hence the death of God can be understood as the very center of this absolute self-negation, a death of God that is not only the consummation of history but is the final actuality of every act or realization of both history and consciousness, an actuality in which "Substance" becomes "Subject," but only by way of an absolute transfiguration of itself, a transfiguration ultimately occurring in its every act and movement. Accordingly, the death of God occurs in substance itself, and occurs as the inevitable realization of substance itself, a realization in which "Substance" becomes "Subject," and if this is the realization of totality itself, it is the realization of an absolutely self-emptying or self-negating totality.

Hegel's thinking of totality goes far beyond every other thinking of totality, whether Eastern or Western; no other thinking comprehends so many dimensions or modes or topics of thinking, yet all are comprehended by a method of thinking that is an absolute self-negation or self-emptying. Now if this can be understood as ultimately deriving from the death of God, or the absolute self-negation or self-emptying

of the Godhead, then Hegel's thinking as a whole is a theological thinking, the only theological thinking that is a total thinking. This is the
ultimate theological challenge of Hegel's thinking, one that has certainly never been met by any existing theology, but one that nonetheless
poses the greatest possible challenge to theology. Of course, innumerable enactments of the death or ending of Hegelian thinking have
occurred, but these are inseparable from the ending of philosophical
thinking itself, and if it is Heidegger who realizes this most profoundly, it is Heidegger who is perhaps our closest counterpart to Hegel, a
Heidegger who effects an absolute contraction or diminution of totality itself, and who perhaps only thereby becomes a genuine theological
thinker. This is the Heidegger who refuses to think about God, except
for the purely negative thinking about God occurring in *Beiträge*; but it
is also the Heidegger who is a genuine apocalyptic thinker, and above
all so in *Beiträge*, and if only here Heidegger is a rebirth of Hegel.

While Heidegger is also a deeply historical thinker, and is so as
is no other twentieth-century philosopher, historical and apocalyptic
thinking are truly conjoined in both Hegel and Heidegger, so much so
as to raise the question whether historical and apocalyptic thinking are
ultimately inseparable if not finally identical. What we have known as a
historical consciousness is unique to the post-Classical Western world,
and even if it most decisively enters that world through Augustine's
City of God, theology itself has been alienated from genuine historical
thinking; only Hegelian expressions of theology have been genuinely
historical. The alienation of modern theology from biblical criticism
and scholarship is a consequence of its non-historical or anti-historical
ground, and it is not insignificant at this point that theology is likewise alienated from an apocalyptic ground. This is perhaps the most
ultimate crisis of twentieth-century theology, for the twentieth century
opened theologically with a demonstration of the apocalyptic ground
of Jesus and original Christianity, a demonstration that was only
strengthened in the later twentieth century, even as the great body of
theology ever deepened its non-apocalyptic or anti-apocalyptic ground.
Yet if apocalyptic and historical thinking are inseparable, then so too
an anti-apocalyptic thinking will inevitably be an anti-historical thinking, as is nowhere more fully manifest than in the theological world,
and—irony of ironies—it is an anti-apocalyptic thinking that is a truly
unrealistic thinking, as perhaps most manifest in our own time. Could
it be then that precisely a genuine renewal of Hegelian thinking could
be most realistic in our world?

This is perhaps most true for theology; a theological renewal of Hegelian thinking would inevitably be a renewal or even new birth of apocalyptic theological thinking, one with a profoundly historical ground, a ground most decisively manifest in the uniquely modern realization of the death of God. This is the historical context in which we can realize the deeply realistic ground of a uniquely modern apocalyptic theology, one already fully manifest in the *Phenomenology of Spirit*, for this work has a more decisive historical ground than any other philosophical work; even if it is the most abstract and difficult of all philosophical works, it is also our most realistic philosophical work, and precisely because of its profoundly historical ground. Here, an apocalyptic theology is a truly realistic theology, thereby making possible its ultimate enactment of the death of God, a death of God inseparable from a uniquely modern historical ground, and a death of God making possible the most realistic thinking that had ever occurred. How ironical to identify an absolute idealism with an absolute realism, but this was an absolute idealism made possible only by the death of God, and precisely thereby an absolute idealism that is an absolute realism.

Nothing could be more unrealistic than everything we have come to know as theological thinking, and if this too is a consequence of the death of God, Hegel is more purely theological in his thinking than any of our contemporary theologians, and is so in his very understanding of the death of God. For Hegel understands the modern realization of the death of God as a renewal of Crucifixion itself, a crucifixion that is an embodiment of the self-emptying of God enacting the ending of history and making possible the advent of an absolutely new world, the new world that Hegel knew as modernity itself. Yet it is in modernity and only modernity that the historical realization of the death of God occurs, and if this brings to an end every possible conception of God, it does so by realizing an absolutely self-emptying or self-negating Godhead, a self-emptying Godhead absolutely negating or absolutely emptying God Himself, therein negating everything that we have known as the absolutely transcendent and absolutely sovereign God.

Consequently, in the twentieth century it is no longer possible to think God, or not in our major or purer philosophies and theologies. If Whitehead is an exception to this, his is a wholly isolated God, one that does not occur in his thinking until its final and most cryptic expressions. Nothing is more unique in twentieth-century philosophy than the comprehensive absence of God in this thinking. There is, moreover, an absence of any actual understanding of God in twentieth-century theology, as Barth, our most influential theologian, could only create a new dogmatic theology by dissolving all philosophical thinking and understanding. All this is in genuine consistency with Hegelian thinking, and above all with the *Phenomenology of Spirit*, which can be apprehended as our first truly modern theology, and above all so in its enactment of the death of God. This is a death of God that no major twentieth-century philosopher or theologian has truly been able to challenge; indeed, it is only confirmed by our philosophies, most forcefully by Heidegger himself. Here Heidegger is in profound continuity with the *Phenomenology of Spirit*, and it is just in this continuity that we can understand Heidegger theologically.

Meanwhile, the question can be posed whether there has yet been a response to Hegel's actual theological thinking. Certainly Hegel's theological thinking has not been explored from a contemporary perspective; indeed, it can be seen as virgin territory, virtually unknown, though Hegel may be the most creative theological thinker who ever lived. Just as self-negation or self-emptying is the essence of a uniquely Hegelian thinking, so it is the source of the forward movement of history itself, not only making possible a uniquely Hegelian historical thinking, but also a fundamental historical thinking truly alien to our world. Heidegger is perhaps most Hegelian in his deep historical thinking, even if that thinking refuses the forward movement of history, a refusal here arising from a post-Hegelian realization of the death of God, and one inaugurating a total and all-comprehending abyss. While such an abyss is truly alien to Hegelian thinking, and here there is a genuine ground for the anti-Hegelian thinking of our world, it is the ultimately radical Hegelian thinking of Kierkegaard and Marx that first and most decisively realizes that abyss, and if only here Marx and Kierkegaard are inescapable for us all. Yet here there is also an inescapable theological ground for us: an abyss that is an ultimate and absolute abyss, and if only thereby a theological abyss, an abyss that has been fully named only in a Hegelian language, even if in a reverse or inverted Hegelian language.

This language is a truly possible theological language for us, and this is so at a time when all manifest theological language is a deeply conservative language, including the language of our seemingly most radical philosophers, yet it is nonetheless true that the call of a radical theological language is now universally ignored. Does this go hand in hand with a deep turn away from Hegelian thinking, and has there ever been a genuinely Hegelian thinking that is not a radical theological thinking, or not an embodiment of a uniquely modern realization of the death of God? This is just the point at which we are alienated from what is commonly known as Hegelian thinking, a thinking identified as an absolute idealism and prevalent in late nineteenth- and early twentieth-century philosophy, a philosophy that has now come to an end, and that is itself deeply alien to that Hegel who is a profoundly kenotic thinker. Yet this is the Hegel who is most openly a theological thinker, and most so in his very understanding of God, that uniquely Christian God who is only now known as an absolutely kenotic or self-emptying God, as for the first time the Crucified God is known as Godhead itself. How fascinating that this never openly occurs in almost two thousand years of Christian theological thinking. True, Luther profoundly apprehends it, and if this made the Protestant revolution possible, it could never be formulated in a Protestant dogmatics. While Barth perhaps attempted it, he realized it only in his doctrine of election or predestination, wherein alone he can fully and decisively know the Crucified God.

Theologians have long maintained that the Crucified God is truly alien to philosophy, but that is manifestly untrue of Hegel, and profoundly untrue of the deepest and purest Hegelian thinking, or that thinking occurring in the *Phenomenology of Spirit* and the *Science of Logic*. If this thinking is inseparable from a profound and irreversible enactment of the death of God, that death can here be known as a realization of the Crucified God, and a profoundly philosophical realization of that death, one revolutionizing philosophical thinking itself. So too does it revolutionize theological thinking, and all too ironically so as the Crucified God is for the first time fully and decisively realized theologically, that Crucified God who is the uniquely Christian God. Now if Hegel first realizes both philosophically and theologically the uniquely Christian God, is that not a realization of the most comprehensive Godhead ever known or apprehended, so comprehensive that it is open to every possible actualization? Could it be that this is the very point at which Hegelian thinking is most absolutely offensive, most profoundly opposed to every other thinking, precisely in enacting a profound resolution, perhaps the only resolution, of the totality of thinking?

—JUNE 2007

5

NIETZSCHE

Nihilism and the Illusion of Ethics

At the conclusion of *Anna Karenina*, its hero Levin finally realizes a resolution of his quest by coming to understand fully that what good is and what we should live for is truly given to all of us, and each of us has a clear, firm, unquestionable knowledge of this. Yet the good is wholly outside reason, having neither causes nor consequences, for it remains outside every possible chain of causation and can have no possible reward if it is truly good. This answer to Levin's primal question can only be given by life itself, but it is given to everyone, and truly *given*, because it cannot be taken from anything and is beyond any possible understanding. Now this resolution only occurs within the horizon of the ultimacy of death, an ultimate death obsessing Levin throughout his quest, a suffering, death, and eternal oblivion that is certain for us all. Finally, it is impossible to live within the horizon of that destiny, yet Levin's ultimate discovery of goodness and of life does not simply dissolve or obliterate this destiny, and if it does transcend it, it does so only momentarily, or only in a total moment of life itself. That is the total presence that is the resolution of Levin's quest, but it is one wholly beyond any possible understanding, and wholly beyond anything that is not a pure gratuity or pure grace.

Nothing could be a purer assault upon everything that we know as ethics, and in one form or another, this assault occurs in virtually all of the primal expressions of the modern imagination, just as it occurs in the great tragedies throughout our history. Among our major philosophers, only Aristotle could sustain a common ethics, which is perhaps a decisive reason why he so purely distinguishes thinking from praxis, and if that is a distinction that breaks down through the course of modernity, it is modernity that culminates in a dissolution of ethical thinking, or a dissolution of all established or manifest ethical understanding. At this crucial point, modern philosophy and the modern imagination are in full correlation with each other, which is one reason why each is so distant from both our institutions and our common life, as most concretely manifest in our religious institutions and our religious life. Never before has our religious life been so far removed both from the imagination and from critical thinking, and if our theologies now threaten to collapse into ethical theologies and ethical theologies alone, such ethical theologies are not only theoretically vacuous but removed from all possible actual engagement with the world. Hence our common ethical language is an actually empty language, or can have impact only when it embodies a reactionary or repressive tradition, with the consequence that it commonly serves our most reactionary or most repressive forces. So it is becoming increasingly manifest that nothing is more difficult for us than an actual ethical language, or an ethical language that could now be a truly liberating language, or a language actually opposing and reversing those dark and alien powers that are now so engulfing us.

Here, perhaps, we are most in need of a Socratic wisdom, a genuine recognition that we do not know what ethics is, that our presumed understanding of ethics is at bottom a deep ignorance, and that our ethical teachers or masters are little better than Sophists. It is all too significant that historically our great creators of ethics have initiated their callings by assaulting or dissolving all given or manifest or established ethics, turning all such categories upside down, with the consequence that our ethical revolutions have been inseparable from an ethical anarchism, or a sweeping away of all established ethical principles. The very idea that there is a common and universal ethics is in this perspective truly illusory, and not only illusory but an ultimate ground of established order and authority, or that ground which is the source of impotence and repression. For to believe that there is a universal ethics is to be opposed to any possible ethical revolution, or any possible ultimate ethical transformation, that very transformation that a Buddha or a Christ embodies, and a transformation that is the deepest challenge to the absoluteness of the given. Our common ethics sanctions that given, and sanctions it by presuming that a common ethics is a genuine and ultimate ethics, a way that is *the* way, and hence a way precluding the possibility of any other way. Thereby the possibility is precluded that there could be any world other than our world, or any world other than the given world, or any world not in genuine continuity with this world.

Now it is just a common or an apparent ethics that defies all critical understanding, or all critical understanding that does not dissolve or reverse such ethics, just as imaginatively such an ethics can only be enacted as a truly negative or alien ethics, as an ethics ultimately dissolving or reversing life itself. Our great liberators throughout history have liberated us from just such ethics, nevertheless such negated ethics have returned again and again, and returned so as to obliterate those revolutions that they reverse, as is most decisively manifest in the Christian world. For there is no greater mystery in Christianity than the mystery of Jesus, a mystery not only of who Jesus is, but the mystery of that way that he embodied and enacted, a way simply inexplicable within the horizon of everything that we know as ethics, and a way disenacting every possible ethics. This is clearest in the call to perfection in the Sermon on the Mount, a perfection transcending every possible obedience but thereby disenacting every possible impotence or passivity, for this is a perfection that is a fullness or totality of life itself. Hence it is wholly closed to everything that we know as ethics, and is so if only because no obligation is possible here, and with that closure the imperative itself disappears or dissolves, and dissolves if only because of the advent of a life that is all in all.

Even if the Sermon on the Mount is a construct of the author or authors of the Gospel according to Matthew, it is accepted virtually everywhere as a pure expression of the ethics of Jesus. Yet this ethics is not simply or only an ethics, it is an eschatological or apocalyptic ethics, hence a Kingdom ethics, or an ethics calling for an enactment of the Kingdom of God. And this call is the very opposite of a pure or absolute imperative, for it is a call embodying an absolutely new and total indicative, that indicative which is the Kingdom of God, and thereby a pure indicative that is simultaneously a pure imperative. Hence this indicative is wholly other than a Pauline "law," but rather its very opposite, for it is the absolute grace of the Kingdom of God, one enacting itself in our very midst. Indeed, the hearer of this new

Torah becomes new in that very hearing, for the hearers of these commands are declared to be fortunate or blessed as the poor and the pure, the truly merciful who are recipients of this ultimate gift, and thereby themselves enactors of these commands, commands that in their enactment become grace itself.

There can be no doubt that an absolute imperative is enacted here, and in its purest form occurs in this summary of the Sermon on the Mount: "Be perfect, therefore, as your heavenly Father is perfect" (Matt. 5:48). Nothing could be further from Torah itself, nor is it possible to imagine such an absolute command as a new Torah, for it is absolute command itself that undergoes a self-negation or self-emptying here, and does so by demanding a perfection that is perfection itself. This cannot possibly be understood as a wholeness or maturity, as is manifest in virtually all of the specific commands in the Sermon on the Mount; it is far rather a perfection that is holiness itself, a pure holiness that *is* the holiness of Abba or Father. This could only be an absolute blasphemy from the perspective of a Torah Judaism, and even if the Gospel according to Matthew reflects a Jewish Christianity that is truly committed to Torah, this only deepens the blasphemy occurring here, as the hearer is called to become the holiness of God. Surely such an absolute commandment is a disenactment of commandment itself, or rather a pure reversal of the absolute imperative, one in which the commanded is called upon to become commander, or to become the source of commandment itself, which is an inevitable consequence of becoming the holiness of God. Can this be genuinely meaningful at all, or is it meaningful only as a disenactment or a deconstruction of the holiness of God, of the absolute sovereignty and transcendence of God, or a reversal of that sovereignty and transcendence so as to make possible an absolutely new life?

Only in this sense does this new Moses enact a new Torah, a new Torah that is a new covenant or new testament, an absolutely new Torah that *is* the Kingdom of God. This is just why the absolute imperative and the absolute indicative are one and the same in this new Torah, as commandment itself passes into its very opposite, for now there is no difference whatsoever between the commander and the commanded, or not insofar as the commandment is exercised or enacted. And it is enacted by being heard, or insofar as it is actually heard, a hearing that is doing itself, so that the hearer of this command becomes truly blessed or truly holy, and truly holy by embodying this ultimate grace or gift. Thus the receiver of this gift is finally nothing but this gift, as everything else becomes invisible and unheard, or unheard and invisible apart from the total presence of this gift, a total presence that is finally the self-negation or self-emptying of everything but this gift. This is the self-emptying that enacts obedience to this command, an obedience that is the precise opposite of an interior obedience, for now an original interior that is subject to obedience passes away in the very reception of this gift, a reception ending the ultimate ground of every actual interior.

Paul could deeply know this gift of obedience as a gift ending every possible "law"—a law that was nonetheless almost immediately resurrected in Christianity, not least so by Paul himself, and if this effected the greatest transformation of a new cultural world ever realized in history, thereby the way of Jesus became the mystery of mysteries, and most so within Christianity itself. As a consequence, the virtually innumerable ethical ways of Christianity are simultaneously this-worldly and otherworldly at once, a dichotomy at the very center of historical Christianity, one embodying the world as world deeply within Christianity, as is fully reflected in every actual Christian ethics. Even the most worldly expressions of Christianity reflect an inversion of otherworldliness, and the otherworldly expressions of Christianity in the sheer totality of their otherworldliness reflect the profound impact of the world as world. Here ethics itself is inseparable from the horizon of the world, and the secularization of this ethics realized a worldly power transcending every other power. But that power, too, is inseparable from its opposite, as manifest in our contemporary world, a world in which passivity and impotence are all in all, and in which ethics is either unmanifest and invisible or confined within an all too solitary or sectarian realm.

Christians often affirm that the Sermon on the Mount can only be practiced by the perfect, or practiced by the "saints"; this was once a common justification for the monastic vocation, just as it was also a justification for the founding of otherworldly sects, and it even created the possibility of a new worldliness in which no true or ultimate ethical praxis is possible. Such worldliness often goes hand in hand with an otherworldliness, and in our world the most blatant or pure worldliness is often deeply allied with the most otherworldly movements and sects, sects distancing themselves from all modern culture and society, yet even thereby realizing a new and overwhelming worldliness. Can this be a consequence of the call to perfection in the Sermon on the Mount?

It is remarkable that there has been so little philosophical commentary on the Sermon on the Mount, although Kant's second critique in its centering upon the absolute imperative could be understood as a profound philosophical misunderstanding of this discourse, and a misunderstanding becoming ever more pervasive in full modernity, as ethics itself becomes ever more fully formal and abstract and ever more decisively divorced from actuality itself. Yet the Sermon on the Mount has continually been renewed in our deepest ethical engagements, and this owing to its profoundly apocalyptic ground, making possible its renewal in apocalyptic moments or apocalyptic situations. Certainly the gift of this discourse cannot be received apart from an ultimate uprooting, one shattering every given consciousness and world. Only that shattering makes possible an opening to this gift, an opening realizing the advent of a second Adam or a new humanity, and a new humanity only insofar as it is open to this ultimate grace. Hence Kingdom of God can only be heard by this new humanity, and passes into its opposite when heard by an old humanity, a humanity closed to that absolute command which ultimately inverts or reverses itself, and does so in the very command to be perfect.

Now, just as only the Christian world has realized a total empire, an empire grounded in a truly new obedience that is internal and external simultaneously, a Christian empire that can be understood as an essential and necessary seed of uniquely twentieth-century totalitarianism, the Christian world has also called forth a unique worldliness, a worldliness whose immense pragmatic power is inseparable from a truly a-ethical ground, a ground wholly divorced from all ethical traditions and ethical ways. We know the hypocrisies in our world of a business ethics, or a legal ethics, or a political ethics, but we also know that such hypocrisy is inescapable for us, and inseparable from the pragmatic power of our world, and if that is the greatest pragmatic power in the history of the world, is it too a consequence of the call to perfection?

Certainly a profound crisis in ethics is manifest today, one surely going beyond every previous ethical crisis, and doing so in its sheer universality, a universality penetrating everywhere. This is a crisis that the deepest expressions of full modernity have known as a consequence of the death of God, a death of God that is not simply the eclipse of God, but the dissolution of all actual transcendence, or the transformation of transcendence itself into an absolute immanence. Thereby the ultimate ground of every established ethics collapses, every possible imperative becomes wholly empty or unreal, or simply becomes identical with the given itself. Then the imperative is truly indistinguishable from the indicative, such that ethics is indistinguishable from life itself, and the degree of ethics or the depth of ethics is simply identical with the depth of life, as ethics loses every sign and mark of its original or established identity and thus becomes unrecognizable as ethics. Hence ours is at bottom an a-ethical world, one stripped of every possible ethical ground, and this not in its periphery but in its depths, depths now wholly engulfing us, and engulfing us as an ultimate emptiness or ultimate void.

Now, in this situation to attempt to practice ethics is finally to move in a circle, a circle in which we can never move beyond our given condition, can never actually do the good, or never actually do anything at all. And this is because now there can be no good or no goal beyond our immediate condition, or no such goal and no such good that can be anything more than fantasy or illusion, because now all actual transcendence has disappeared or has been wholly transformed into a new and final immanence. All too strangely, this condition parallels the ways of Jesus and Gautama, for here the imperative also disappears, disappearing in that perfection enacted by Jesus and that enlightenment enacted by Gautama, and if these ways revolutionized the ethics of their worlds, our ethical impotence or ethical passivity is revolutionizing the ethics of our world, and doing so by virtually bringing it to an end. While this is a condition that is publicly ignored, a deep disquiet is nevertheless at hand, for just as a genuine ethical discourse has disappeared in all of our public worlds, our private worlds are profoundly threatened as never before, and ultimately threatened by the comprehensive advent of a new and total technology.

Perhaps what is most fascinating about our condition is that there is apparently so little effort to transcend it, for as opposed to our situation only two generations ago, one can now discover virtually no attempts either in thinking or the imagination to enter truly new worlds, and if these are nonetheless occurring they are all too invisible and unheard, as is most manifestly true in the realm of ethics itself. One is tempted to think that this field has become so banal that it repulses everyone with either a mind or an imagination, but far more than that is at hand, for above all other discourse it is ethical discourse that has become most challenging or most impossible for us, and just as this is a truly new condition, it is the clearest and most open symptom of that nihilism that is engulfing us. Both Kierkegaard and Nietzsche fully foresaw this, and if Heidegger is the greatest philosopher of the twentieth century, at no point is he more prescient than here, for Heidegger could know and enact our destiny as a nihilistic destiny, even if at bottom this is an apocalyptic enactment. But the truth is that apocalyptic enactments have always brought an end to every ethical horizon; this is clearest in Paul in the ancient world, and in Nietzsche in the modern world, though such apocalyptic disenactments are inseparable from their opposite, the calling forth of an absolutely new ethical world. If this occurred in Buddhism and Christianity in the ancient world, it could occur only by way of a total disruption, and a total disruption of ethics itself, or of every ethics manifest and real apart from these truly new and revolutionary ways.

Hence we need not necessarily despair at our new condition, as it could make possible a new world or a new life for us, but only insofar as we lose every illusion about our condition, and above all surrender that illusion of ethics which appears to be so necessary for us. It is highly significant that the one major thinker in our world who created or realized a genuine ethics, Levinas, could do so only by enacting an absolutely primordial ethics, one wholly and totally removed from our world. Is only an absolutely otherworldly ethics possible for us? Is that the consequence of our new and nihilistic condition, and is even Nietzsche's Dionysian ethics wholly otherworldly for us or absolutely distant from our world? The truth is that a genuinely otherworldly ethics is not an ethics at all, or not an ethics that can actually be practiced in the world or can actually affect its world. Or, insofar as this occurs, it would be invisible in the world itself and wholly without any manifest pragmatic effects, without any transformations that could actually be manifest as transformations. Has there ever been another time in our history when we have been so deeply drawn to an otherworldly ethics, and is this a decisive sign of the unreality of every manifest ethics in our world, or of every possible ethics that could be an actual ethics for us? And is this yet another condition impelling us to a radically new ethical quest, one so new that it would not even appear as an ethical quest, and would perhaps transcend all possible ethical language?

Yet Gautama's and Jesus's language wholly transcended the ethical languages of their worlds; each could be attacked as ultimate enemies of ethics itself, just as each would no doubt have been identified as a nihilist if nihilism had been known in their worlds. Accordingly, it is Nietzsche, our deepest nihilistic thinker, who can be identified by so many as our greatest ethical thinker, a Nietzsche whose only genuine philosophical counterpart is Spinoza, a Spinoza who without being named as such was known as our deepest nihilist until Nietzsche; a Spinoza who is nevertheless the most totally ethical thinker in Western history. While it is true that Nietzsche has been renewed as an ethical thinker for us, if only in our most radical circles, no such renewal has occurred of Spinoza, perhaps because this would be a far more radical project, or perhaps because Spinoza is far more distant from our world than is Nietzsche, and most distant as our most comprehensively ethical thinker. Yes, ethics is our most unknown language, that language which is most alien to us, and perhaps most alien when it is seemingly most real, or when it is apparently most fully at hand. That at-handedness is a primal source of our passivity, and our impotence too, for here illusion consumes us, and consumes us because we are absorbed by a wholly empty language, or a language actual only in its debilitating effect.

No one so deeply unveils illusion as does the Buddha, and even if this unveiling occurs in innumerable forms, it is Buddhism that has most profoundly drawn forth the illusion of everything that is manifestly real, and this comprehends all possible ethical language. Here, a pure silence is all in all, a liberating silence, and one most clearly liberating in its dissolution of illusion, and if this is a dissolution of all possible selfhood, it is also thereby a dissolution of every possible center. Yet Buddhism can critically be known as the most deeply ethical of all historical ways, the one most actually effecting a total self-giving, and one drawing forth totality itself as a total emptiness which is a total compassion. Could it be that the deepest ethical way is wholly unmanifest as an ethical way, or wholly unreal in everything that we can recognize or know as ethics, or wholly unspeakable in everything that is possible as an ethical language? Buddhism inevitably poses such questions, but these questions also resonate with our contemporary condition, a condition in which an actual ethics is seemingly impossible, but one that may nevertheless make possible a truly new even if unnameable ethics. Perhaps such an unnameability is a real hope for us, and if our language is the most actual source of our illusion, and our ethical language the most actual source of our ethical illusion, then the seeming impossibility of a genuinely ethical language for us could be a decisive sign of a truly new possibility, and as such one wholly absent from all of our horizons.

Yet as Buddhism makes fully manifest, it is extraordinarily difficult to be liberated from deep illusion, and not simply difficult but virtually impossible, or impossible in our common or given condition. That is the condition that Buddhism inverts, or turns upside down, but is such an inversion possible for us, and is it possible wholly to invert or reverse our ethical language and our ethical consciousness? This is seemingly accomplished by Nietzsche, and by Spinoza too, but apparently no one can actually accept such a total inversion, or can accept it by actually willing or living it, and living it in its totality. Nietzsche could issue such a call only by way of his imitation or repetition of Jesus, but this is a forward-moving repetition in a Kierkegaardian sense, for it is not a backward movement to Jesus, not an attempt to recover the original Jesus, but far rather a reenactment of the revolutionary Jesus in our world, or in a world in which God is dead. Hence it could occur only as a wholly blasphemous repetition, and as a total blasphemer Nietzsche is rivaled only by Joyce, but it is just such blasphemy that is necessary for this repetition, and necessary if only to effect that profound shock apart from which no actual reversal could occur. Of course, such a reversal can issue and has issued in ultimate pathologies, in absolutely destructive and self-destructive acts, acts that are unique to our world and which embody a truly unique horror. But we can observe such destructiveness and self-destructiveness in Christian history itself, a history seemingly made possible only by Jesus, and yet a history unrivaled by any other history in its profound negativity.

Nietzsche knew this negativity more profoundly than any other thinker with the exception of Hegel, yet this is a negativity by which Nietzsche can be identified as a genuinely Christian thinker, and most clearly so in his ultimate reversal of Christian ethics, a reversal only possible by occurring in the very center of that ethics. Here Nietzsche surpasses even Spinoza, and if he echoes Spinoza in his enactment of an absolute Yes-saying, he goes beyond him by transforming thinking into willing itself, and an absolute willing, even if the absolute willing of the Will to Power. Yet here "power" is an inversion or reversal of every common or manifest meaning of power, and is so if only because it is a consequence of absolute will, an absolute will only historically manifest in the uniquely Christian God, whose death Nietzsche could know as the ultimate source of an absolutely new will, one apocalyptically new as an absolutely immanent will. Inevitably, there is a universal misunderstanding of Nietzsche's Will to Power, and not least so in Heidegger himself, a misunderstanding proceeding from an absent theological ground, for here Will to Power is not only a consequence of the death of God but is itself an absolute reversal of the absolutely transcendent God, a reversal only made possible by that absolute death. Hence it is a reversal of the absolute power of God, one releasing an absolute self-emptying or kenosis, but as opposed to Buddhism, this is a wholly actual self-emptying, an actuality that Nietzsche names as Eternal Recurrence or the Will to Power.

If Nietzsche, along with Kierkegaard, is our greatest ironist, he is nowhere more ironical than in his naming of the Will to Power, one inverting every possible biological or physical power, and inverting it in response to an absolutely new life, a life only possible as a consequence of the death of God. Now that is the death of an absolutely sovereign transcendent power, but this death is not a dissolving death, not simply an annihilating death, but an absolutely transforming death, and a death transforming absolute transcendence into absolute immanence. One can gain an understanding of this by recalling Nietzsche's identification of the Christian God as a truly nihilistic God, the deification of nothingness, but it is an absolute reversal of that "nothingness" that realizes the Will to Power, and only in the perspective of the Will to Power can the Christian God or absolute transcendence be known as an actual nothingness, a nothingness that is the consequence of the death of God. Thereby the death of God issues in a new and absolute nihilism, a nihilism that is our inescapable destiny, and a nihilism that is the very arena of the Will to Power and Eternal Recurrence.

Accordingly, an ethics that could be an ethics for us will inevitably be a nihilistic ethics, at the very least an ethics directed to a nihilistic condition, hence an ethics employing a nihilistic language, one already present in the revolutionary imaginative languages of late modernity, languages which themselves are ultimately ethical, even if their ethical meaning can only be called forth by a radical hermeneutics. Joyce is here the paradigmatic model, and above all his *Finnegans Wake*, and if this is a radically new language that is nevertheless the language of everybody, it is also a kenotic or self-emptying language, and even is so as a nihilistic language. Thereby it truly parallels Buddhism, or any Buddhism that could be real to the contemporary mind, but so likewise does it parallel or even renew the revolutionary Jesus, and most decisively so in its actual enactment of self-emptying. But this is not a self-emptying that could be manifest as such to our common or our given world, not a self-emptying that could appear as ethical to us, but far rather a self-emptying that is a nihilistic self-emptying, and most clearly so in its truly chaotic language. Once again Buddhism can be a way into this language, and can be so in its enactment of a pure and total selflessness, a selflessness that can be apprehended as embodied in Here Comes Everybody, and can be so because this everybody is a decentered everybody, an everybody who is everyone and no one at once.

Now, we can know *Finnegans Wake* as an ultimately ethical work only in revolutionizing our understanding of ethics; here all our ethical categories must undergo a fundamental inversion or reversal, and even the ethical act itself will become the very reversal of its given or common identity, and will do so because now an ethical act is indistinguishable from any other act, and is so just because it is wholly decentered. There is a truly and absolutely new universality in *Finnegans Wake* just as there is in Nietzsche's fully mature thinking, a universality in which everything passes into everything else but only by way of a total self-emptying or a total decentering, a decentering or total reversal of every given or common identity. Yes, this is nihilism, but it is a holy nihilism, or a liberating nihilism, and most manifestly so in liberating its enactor from ethics itself, or from every ethics that is manifest to us, or every ethics that is an imperative ethics, or every ethics that is ethics and ethics alone. Already Spinoza accomplished this, and did so as a totally ethical thinker, but that is just an ethics in which every common ethics disappears, and disappears in that totality which is an ethical totality, but is only a totality by the disappearance of ethics itself. No longer is ethics a distinct or distinguishable realm, and no longer is it opposed to anything else or in opposition to anything at all, for no longer is it "ethics" or anything that we can name or know as ethics.

If Nietzsche could unveil ethics as our deepest and our purest illusion, or as our most destructive and self-destructive ground, this nonetheless made possible a radically new ethics, but a new ethics that is unknowable and unnameable as ethics. Indeed, it is the very opposite of everything that we know as ethics, hence Nietzsche's naming of absolute Yes-saying as Eternal Recurrence or the Will to Power, and his evocation of a noble morality as opposed to a slave morality, a slave morality that is quite simply our morality, or our given morality, and a noble morality that is the morality of the Will to Power. But the Will to Power is not the will to power; it is not anything that can be known as power to those who are imprisoned by the impotence of *ressentiment* and therefore can only know power as a wholly disembodied or alien power. Power, for the mature Nietzsche, is the power of the will, and it is released only by Yes-saying or by an absolute affirmation, just as it is dissolved or reversed by No-saying, hence Nietzsche's discovery of *ressentiment*. This is a discovery made possible only by the death of God, only by the advent of an absolutely immanent power, an immanent power reversing every possible transcendent power, and an immanent power fully incarnate in the body and the world. *Ressentiment* is the consequence of a turning away from or a repression of that power, thus it is the very opposite of the Will to Power, and as such is the very reversal of will itself.

Nothing is more difficult for us to apprehend than an actual ethics of what Nietzsche knows as the Will to Power, but once we understand that Will to Power can only be the very opposite of everything that is given or manifest as "will to power," then we know that such an ethics can only be a kenotic or self-emptying ethics, or an ethics truly coincident or parallel with that ethics that Nietzsche himself called forth in *The Anti-Christ* as being enacted by Jesus. Nonetheless it would be wholly invisible as ethics from every given or common perspective, indeed, the very opposite of what we have known and named as ethics, so that it would be wholly illusory as an actual ethics, and only manifest as being truly destructive of ethics itself. Thus it could not possibly appear as an ethics, but only as an anti-ethics, the deepest possible anti-ethics, hence it would or could be known not only as the ethics of the Anti-Christ, but as the purest Satanic ethics. This, of course, is just how the ethics of Nietzsche is commonly known, but is this not at bottom how we apprehend the ethics of Jesus, an ethics wholly removed from every point of contact with actuality itself, yet not simply an illusory ethics, or a pure innocence, but far rather an ethics turning the world or actuality upside down, and therefore a purely anarchistic or purely deconstructive ethics.

If it is Blake who most purely and most comprehensively envisioned how "innocence" is inevitably and necessarily transformed into "experience," this is now manifest in the ethical realm itself; and if there is no genuine ethics of innocence in our world, we are overwhelmed by an ethics of experience, an ethics deeply sanctioning experience, thereby reversing every possible ethics of innocence, thus realizing an ethics that is the very opposite of any possible innocence. If this is an all too worldly ethics, and one fully actual in our world, it is just thereby profoundly distant from an anarchistic or apocalyptic ethics, profoundly distant from the ethics of both Nietzsche and Jesus, and if only in that perspective the ethics of Jesus and the ethics of Nietzsche stand together. Yet they also stand together in being truly and ultimately revolutionary, in being at the furthest possible distance from everything that is given and manifest in their worlds, hence they not only demand but enact total transformations of those worlds, and do so not in their peripheries but in their deepest centers. Indeed, is Nietzsche the only thinker in our world who can truly open us to the revolutionary Jesus, and do so precisely by his most revolutionary thinking, and if that is a thinking in which everything that we know as ethics becomes invisible, is this a thinking truly open to the horizon of the ethics of Jesus?

Just as it is only by a fundamental mispronunciation or misapprehension that we can actually speak of the ethics of Nietzsche, is this not equally true of our attempts to speak of the ethics of Jesus? Is any such language actually possible for us? Or could its possibility be established for us if we would first accept the deep illusion of all of our given or manifest language about the ethics of Jesus, indeed, also of all of our manifest ethical language of whatever kind? For our only ethical language is a common language; here we are bereft of all technical or sophisticated language, and to the extent that this occurs in our philosophical and theological ethics, it occurs simply to clarify an ethical problem or dilemma, and not to resolve the problem itself. Yet if our common ethical language is finally incapable of being an ethical language for us, is this not a summons to a radical new quest for us, and a summons inseparable from a radical and even absolute ethical crisis?

Perhaps it is only by a real acceptance of illusion that we can become open to Jesus. Clearly this is true for any possible opening on our part to the Buddha, and not simply because the domain of the Buddha appears to be infinitely distant from our own, but because any actual way of liberation is vastly distant from us, and because our very language, our given and common language, is a primary source of such distance. There is a strange and paradoxical affirmation of illusion in Buddhism and Christianity alike, one in which an ultimate illusion is identified as samsara or old aeon, and only the dissolution or reversal of that illusion makes liberation possible. Just as Mahayana Buddhism identifies samsara and nirvana, apocalyptic Christianity celebrates that new aeon which is now becoming all in all. And just as the depths of samsara are known only through enlightenment, the depths of sin are known only through grace. So, too, redemption is possible only through the actual negation or reversal of illusion or sin, and in Christianity, sin or original sin can be known as a *felix culpa*, a fortunate fall apart from which neither redemption nor apocalypse is possible. In this perspective, it would not be gratuitous to speak of our ethical crisis as a *felix culpa*, one making possible an actual confrontation with our ultimate dilemma, a condition too often disguised in our histories and traditions, and most disguised in our philosophies and theologies in their all too worldly institutional expressions. Here, genuine nihilism can be known as a liberating nihilism, one liberating us from ultimate illusions, and doing so by way of an absolute negation that negates illusion too, and even if no resolution is possible in nihilism itself, an ultimate clearing does occur, and a clearing essential to any actual possibility of liberation.

—SEPTEMBER 2004

6

HEIDEGGER

Ereignis and the Nothing

One of the deepest mysteries of the Western world is the mystery of nothingness, a nothingness here known as being both illusory and real, illusory as an ontological nothingness, but real as evil and death. An actual nothingness does not enter philosophical thinking until German Idealism, when it makes possible that absolute negation which Hegel so profoundly enacts, just as it makes possible the first philosophical understanding of a real and actual evil. While such an understanding is implicit in Augustine's truly new understanding of evil, Augustine's Neoplatonism foreclosed the possibility of a philosophical understanding of that pure negativity, and at this point not even Aquinas could transcend such a Neoplatonism. This does not occur historically until the full advent of the modern world, as most decisively occurring in Luther, and then it occurs only by an ending of philosophical theology, an ending deeply renewed by Barth in the twentieth century, a Barth who could know the triumph of Christ as an ultimate and final ending of the Nihil, and a Nihil that is real if only in that ending (*Church Dogmatics* 3:3). Not until Barth does a major theologian speak of the Nihil or the Nothing, a language only possible after the collapse of scholasticism, and this occurs in a new world in which there is an ultimate epiphany of evil and nothingness, one realizing itself in the Holocaust, and in the wake of the Holocaust could it be anything but a pure blasphemy to speak of evil as the privation of the good?

Heidegger, in his book on Schelling, regarded Schelling's *Philosophical Investigations into the Essence of Human Freedom* (1809) as the acme of the metaphysics of German Idealism, as even the essential core of all Western metaphysics can be discerned in complete clarity in this treatise, and here one may most clearly discover that all philosophy is finally "ontotheology," or is ontological and theological simultaneously. Here, a pure philosophical theological thinking is a thinking of absolute freedom, one present only in God, and present only in the becoming of that Godhead which strives against the "darkness" or "evil" of itself. While this is a darkness that only truly enters philosophical thinking in German Idealism, it is a darkness that Schelling can speak of as "that within God which is not *God himself*" (*Philosophical Investigations* §359), but is the very ground of God's existence, releasing a primordial longing to give birth to itself. Here, Schelling is under the deep impact of Eckhart and Böhme, and can even speak of that "Nothing" which has long since been the cross of reason, a Nothing that is the second principle of darkness or the spirit of evil, for it transcends that dark principle which had made possible the original creation. In God, too, there would be a depth of darkness if he did not make it his own and unite it to himself, and it is this union that makes possible both the love and the glorification of God (§399). This is that love that is the absolute freedom of God, but it is finally a human freedom too, or is so when we "exist in God" (§347), an existence here embodying the apocalyptic birth of a new world, a world calling forth a truly new God, a God who had never been truly thought before.

Hegel's science of logic is the purest and most comprehensive system of thinking that has evolved in the Western world, and if logic is the realm of pure thought, here this realm is truth as it is, without veil, and in its own absolute nature, as Hegel declares in its introduction, so that the content of pure logic is the exposition of God as he is in his eternal essence before the creation. Yet nothing is more elusive in the *Science of Logic* than the identity of God, a God or Godhead that is a pure and absolute kenosis or self-emptying, and a Godhead perhaps most elusive in what is here enacted as absolute beginning. Now absolute beginning in its very identity of beginning is the unity of being and nothing, a union in which being and nothing are distinguished from each other in the beginning, and this is the distinction that is absolutely essential to beginning itself. For the beginning as such is only on the way to being, a being that is the "other" of non-being, therefore the being embodied in the beginning is a being that removes itself from non-being, or that negates non-being as something opposed to and other than itself. That negation is genesis or the beginning, and therefore the opposites of being and non-being are united in that beginning, a beginning that is the undifferentiated unity of being and nothing. But absolute beginning embodies mediation within itself, a mediation between the opposites of being and nothing, and a mediation that is realized in the knowledge that being *is* nothing. This realization is the realization that pure being, or being without any further differentiation, is in fact "nothing," neither more nor less than nothing. Only the vanishing of that pure being and pure nothing is the advent of becoming, a becoming that is the unity of being and nothing; not a unity that abstracts from being and nothing, but a determinate unity in which there is both being and nothing.

Only in the *Science of Logic* does an actual nothing enter pure thinking, and nothing is newer here than the thinking of an actual nothingness, but this can be understood as the consequence of the advent of a truly new world, and one inseparable from a fully actual Nihil or Nothing. Goethe's *Faust* is that imaginative work which had the greatest impact upon the modern German mind, and if the Faust myth was born in the very advent of modernity, it enacted a uniquely Western damnation, a damnation that is the consequence of the will to power, and a damnation which Goethe gave his deepest power to reversing. This occurs in the second part of Goethe's ultimate drama, as the passionately subjective Faust of the first part ever more fully realizes a trans-subjective and trans-individual power, a power that alone can reverse the damnation of Faust. This most decisively occurs in the first act of the tragedy's second part, occurring in a descent into the realm of the Mothers in the "Dark Gallery," and Mephistopheles reveals to Faust that these goddesses are enthroned in sublime solitude, a solitude where there is neither space nor time. Indeed, there is no way to this solitude, a solitude that is a pure void, and one that Mephistopheles identifies as the Nothing. Faust accepts a summons to this Nothing, and can even declare: "In deinem Nichts hoff ich das All zu finden" (*Faust* 2:6256: "I hope to find the All in your Nothing"). If that All is truly the Nothing of Mephistopheles, a realization of that All will be a triumphant fulfillment of the wager of the first part (2:1692–1706), a fulfillment reversing the damnation of Faust.

Now a descent occurs into the unbound realms of form, realms that have long since been dissipated, and a descent that Mephistopheles can identify as ascent, and only when Faust has arrived in the deepest abyss will he behold the radiant glow of the Mothers and encounter that ultimate transformation that is eternal re-creation. As Faust declares, the Mothers have their throne in boundlessness, a boundlessness that is the womb of all and everything, and a boundlessness that is the final destiny of Faust. This destiny is enacted in the conclusion of the drama when Faust as Faust disappears, and disappears by way of an ultimate union with the Eternal Feminine, an Eternal Feminine that is the resolution of those deep feminine powers occurring throughout the drama, but that are only unveiled in Faust's descent into the realm of the Mothers. These powers are embodied in the Catholic Mother of God, who is the one source of salvation in the Christian world, and even as the conclusion of *Faust* is a reenactment of the conclusion of Dante's *Paradiso*, the Mothers are here the one source of salvation, Mothers who are the primordial source of the Virgin and Beatrice alike, the very source that is ecstatically celebrated in the poetry which concludes the drama.

This is an ultimate hymn of celebration intoned by the *chorus mysticus* celebrating that Eternal Feminine drawing us to an absolutely primordial transcendence, a primordial transcendence that is an absolute transfiguration of nothingness itself: "Das Unzulängliche, / Hier wird's Ereignis" (*Faust* 2:12106–12107). Now what is truly empty or deficient or nothing finally becomes *Ereignis*, a holy and disembodied action that is the action of the redeemed Faust. Not until Heidegger is that *Ereignis* born philosophically, in a Heidegger who finally knows an apocalyptic epiphany of *Ereignis* occurring in the very heart of darkness, and occurring only in that final apocalyptic time which is destitute of the holy and is the very consummation of that nihilism which Heidegger knows as the history of Being. Only in the posthumously published *Beiträge* does Heidegger give us a full exposition of *Ereignis*, and here Being itself is finally known as *Ereignis*, and known as such against the transcendent God of Christianity, an *Ereignis* that is "originary history," though only now is that history realizing its fullness in the advent of the utmost remoteness of the "last god," one bringing history to its end. No redemption occurs here, but rather a *letting-into* (*Einsetzung*), a releasement of the originary ownmost in Being itself, and now the empowering of man to God's necessity becomes manifest as *Ereignis* for the first time comes into the open (*Beiträge* §413). An ultimate struggle occurs throughout *Beiträge*, far more so than in any other work of Heidegger, and here he can say that Being has the character of Nothing (*Nichthaft*), for Being needs the *not* to last for the steadfastness of its truth, and that means that it needs the *opposition* of all that is nothing, the "not-being" (§101). There is a deep emphasis here upon the abandonment of Being, one first occurring in Christianity and its absolutely transcendent God, an abandonment in which Being abandons beings, yet one that is now being reversed in the apocalyptic advent of *Ereignis*.

Schelling, Hegel, Nietzsche, and Heidegger are all apocalyptic thinkers, and indeed revolutionary apocalyptic thinkers: thinkers enacting an absolutely new apocalypse inseparable from an absolute Nothing, and an absolutely actual Nothing. As opposed to every possible apophatic thinking, here an absolute Nothing is a totally actual Nothing, as reflected in that nihilism now released in the world. Even if that nihilism is only implicit in Schelling and Hegel, it is fully explicit in Nietzsche and Heidegger, as a new apocalyptic world realizes its own consummation. Already in *Being and Time* Heidegger could deeply know an actual Nothing not only as the source of *Angst*, but as an ultimate ground of freedom itself, but here there is virtually no exposition of the Nothing itself, and in all of Heidegger's vast corpus this only occurs in an abbreviated form in the 1929 lecture "What Is Metaphysics?" Nevertheless, our new nihilism is certainly impossible to understand apart from the advent of a fully actual Nihil, and if it is Nietzsche and Heidegger who most deeply understand our nihilism, it is Heidegger and Nietzsche among our philosophers who most deeply call forth that Nihil, yet here that calling forth is inseparable from an apocalyptic or final redemption. Now just as Nietzsche and Heidegger more deeply call forth an ultimate guilt and fallenness than do any other modern philosophers, so too do they call forth an ultimate redemption, but a redemption absolutely dissociated from everything once known or manifest as "God," and above all dissociated from the uniquely Christian God.

Heidegger is our only truly major philosopher who virtually never speaks of God, yet Heidegger can be understood as the most theological of our twentieth-century philosophers, and perhaps most purely so in his refusal to speak of God, a silence harboring a profound theological understanding and one accepted as such by his theological colleagues. This theological understanding is perhaps most manifest in his apocalyptic thinking, and just as apocalyptic thinking vanished in virtually all modern theological thinking, and vanished most purely in that scholasticism which nourished the young Heidegger, Heidegger's rebellion against theology can be understood as a rebellion against all non-apocalyptic theology, thereby making possible a genuine renewal of apocalyptic theology, one that is realized only as a consequence of the death of God. Heidegger knows that death more deeply than any other twentieth-century thinker, a death that is the ultimate source of our nihilism, yet also a death making possible an apocalyptic *Ereignis*, and an *Ereignis* only realized by the full advent of an absolutely actual Nothing.

Just as Heidegger is our only philosopher capable of speaking in and through the deepest poetry, that poetry in the fullness of modernity and late modernity is a poetry embodying an absolutely actual Nothing. Yet a uniquely modern transfiguration occurs in that poetry, one transfiguring a fully actual and total nothingness, and this is surely an ultimate ground of Heidegger's understanding of *Ereignis*. So, too, our deeply modern poetry is an apocalyptic poetry embodying an absolutely new world, a new world possible only through an apocalyptic ending, which Heidegger could understand as the end of metaphysics or the end of philosophy itself, yet that is an ending making possible an absolutely new beginning. If that beginning is the apocalyptic event of *Ereignis*, it occurs only in the deepest darkness, but a darkness before the dawn, a darkness known by every genuine apocalypticism, but most comprehensively known by a uniquely modern apocalypticism. Thus darkness is absolutely essential to apocalypticism, and if this darkness is most purely embodied in an absolutely actual and absolutely total Nothing, that Nothing is essential to an apocalyptic *Ereignis*, an *Ereignis* wholly unspeakable apart from the Nothing. Why is it that Heidegger would only fully speak of *Ereignis* in a work that he himself would not give to the world or allow to be published until after his death? Is this because it harbors his deepest secret, the secret that he himself is at bottom a theologian?

Ever more fully in recent years we have come to understand how profoundly Heidegger was committed to primordial or original

Christianity, and how he went beyond Kierkegaard in identifying historical Christianity or the historical church as a reversal of that Christianity, as most dramatically stated in his *Parmenides* §3 when he speaks of "Latinization" as the passage of *aletheia* into a Roman imperium, wherein the domination of command passes into the very essence of ecclesiastical dogma. Though philosophers are commonly baffled by what Heidegger might mean by an original or primordial Christianity, this perhaps becomes clearest in his commitment to Paul, and to that Paul who is vastly distant from all established Christianity. For Heidegger discovered the apocalyptic Paul well before this occurred in New Testament scholarship in his 1920 lectures on the phenomenology of religion, and it is perhaps only Pauline language that is real to Heidegger as biblical language, but this is an ultimately apocalyptic language, and the purest apocalyptic language occurring in the Bible as a whole. We know how deeply Heidegger and Bultmann mutually worked on Paul, and Bultmann's re-creation of Paul in *The Theology of the New Testament* (1947) is perhaps our most profound theological interpretation of Paul, which was deeply affected by Heidegger. Heidegger's 1970 preface to his essay "Phenomenology and Theology" (1927) identifies Franz Overbeck as the one who established the world-denying expectation of the end as the basic characteristic of what is primordially Christian. So, too, in that crucial year of 1927 Schweitzer published his great book on Paul, one decisively demonstrating the apocalyptic Paul, thereby truly renewing Overbeck, and as Bultmann's sister once attested (in a personal conversation with me), he was alone among major German New Testament scholars in originally defending Schweitzer's apocalyptic interpretation of Paul.

Now, it is the apocalyptic Paul who is most distant from all established Christian dogma, and Heidegger did not simply become alienated from the Church, but more deeply from its dogma, a purely non-apocalyptic dogma, and one that realized itself only by reversing an originally apocalyptic Christianity. Heidegger understood this more deeply than did the Christian theological world or worlds, and it is crucial to the antithesis which he posited between original Christianity and established Christianity, and just as Heidegger ever more fully became a profoundly apocalyptic thinker, it was just thereby that he truly renewed Schelling, Hegel, and Nietzsche, even if this is not understood by the philosophical world. The truth is that virtually no one today understands either apocalyptic thinking or apocalyptic vision, and even if critical historians almost unanimously know original Christianity as an apocalyptic Christianity, this has had very little effect upon our theological worlds. But it certainly had an enormous impact upon Heidegger, and perhaps nothing more disguises Heidegger's Christian identity than does its deep apocalyptic ground, as all too ironically that which is originally or primordially Christian is vastly distant from or actually reversed in everything that is apparently or manifestly Christian. Not even Kierkegaard or Bultmann so deeply apprehend the antithesis between original Christianity and all established Christianity as does Heidegger, but apart from understanding this antithesis there is no way to a genuine understanding of the theological Heidegger.

While there has been a genuine renewal of Paul in recent Continental philosophy, we have not therein been given a renewed Pauline thinking as so ultimately and profoundly occurs in *Being and Time*, whose understanding of death and guilt and resolution is profoundly Pauline, even if the name of God is unmentioned. While writing *Being and Time*, Heidegger actively participated with Bultmann in a seminar on Paul at Marburg, although this was before an apocalyptic interpretation of Paul was present in New Testament scholarship. A critical apocalyptic interpretation of Paul is not born until Schweitzer's book *The Mysticism of Paul the Apostle* (1927), and here there thereby occurs a dissolution of an established gulf between the historical Jesus and the historical Paul. Schweitzer calls forth a Pauline "co-experiencing" of crucifixion and resurrection from which ethics immediately and directly results, but this is an apocalyptic ethics only made possible by the advent of the Kingdom of God, and an apocalyptic ethics wholly other than all established ethics.

Could a Pauline "co-experiencing" of crucifixion and resurrection be an ultimate ground of Heidegger's thinking, one largely disguised in Heidegger's own language, but nonetheless occurring in his radical understanding of *Angst*, death, fallenness, and resolution, thereby giving us a truly new ethics, and a truly new Pauline ethics? Does the common judgment that Heidegger is a non-ethical or a-ethical thinker proceed from a closure to the radically new ethics of *Being and Time*, an ethics that is not only an apocalyptic ethics but one only made possible by the advent of a total judgment, a judgment finally uprooting every established horizon, and only thereby releasing a truly new Dasein, and a Dasein embodying an ultimate resolution? Now even if this is an absolute resolution discovered by Nietzsche's vision of Eternal Recurrence, Eternal Recurrence as opposed to eternal return is an absolutely forward movement, and therefore an apocalyptic as opposed to a primordial movement, and one reborn in *Being and Time*. Yet Heidegger is a systematic thinker as Nietzsche is not, and just as in "Phenomenology and Theology" Heidegger fully correlates systematic, historical, and practical theology, in his new thinking there occurs a full correlation of historical and ontological thinking, and one that is inescapably an ethical thinking as well, calling for an absolute commitment that even decisively influenced that Levinas who so resisted him. Yet such a commitment is inevitably a theological commitment, as openly manifest in Levinas, and even if Heidegger disguises this, just as he disguises his profound debt to Kierkegaard, Heidegger as a philosophical thinker is even thereby a theological thinker, just as are all his great predecessors.

In this perspective, Heidegger can be known as a genuine Pauline thinker, even at this crucial point more purely Pauline than either Augustine or Luther, and unlike Luther and Augustine, Heidegger can profoundly know the Nothing itself. For even if Augustine and Luther know the Nothing as Satan, the truth is that there is little actual thinking of Satan in Christianity, and imaginatively Satan is not fully envisioned until the advent of the modern world. This occurs most profoundly in Milton's *Paradise Lost*, an epic deeply grounded in the redemptive death of the divinity of the Messiah or the Son of God, and in his *De doctrina Christiana* Milton was the first systematic theologian to know that death. This is that death of God which is at the very center of both Hegel's and Nietzsche's thinking, and it is no less primal in Heidegger's thinking, and nowhere more so than in his enactment of *Ereignis*, an *Ereignis* that is not only the consequence of that death but its apocalyptic consequence, and one bringing history to an end. Yet that ending is apocalypse itself, an apocalypse transfiguring absolute nothingness, a transfiguration impossible apart from that Nihil, or apart from the actual depths of nothingness itself. Hence those depths can be greeted with an absolute affirmation, a "letting-be" that is a response to the ultimate gift of *Ereignis*, and if this is a gift in which Being "gives," Being itself is unspeakable in an opening to this gift, an unspeakability that is an unspeakability of everything we have known as God.

The conclusion of Heidegger's 1964 appendix to "Phenomenology and Theology" (54–62) gives us perhaps his clearest statement of what is commonly understood to be his pagan theology, which is truly ironical since "Phenomenology and Theology" is so decisively a Christian theological enactment. Here, he quotes Rilke's "Gesang ist Dasein" and speaks of poetic thinking as being in the presence of and for "the god," a presence that means simple willingness that wills nothing, and being in the presence of is purely letting the god's presence be said. Now what could be the possible relationship between this "god" and the Crucified God evoked by "Phenomenology and Theology"? Could this be yet another decisive sign of the radical break between the early Heidegger and the later Heidegger, and one that is truly unbridgeable theologically? The fully mature Heidegger refrains from all actual speaking of God, even if he occasionally does speak of "god" or the gods, and perhaps nothing has more comprehensively baffled his interpreters. If Heidegger and Nietzsche are alone among our philosophers in speaking of the gods, it is Nietzsche and not Heidegger who understood the ancient gods, gods who are wholly absent from Heidegger's thinking. Is Heidegger's pagan theology finally then an illusion, and an illusion if only because a truly modern pagan theology is simply unknown, and unknown if only because of the uniquely modern enactment of the death of God, a death wherein deity itself becomes unspeakable?

Yet deity is speakable in the very enactment of the death of God, one alien to all ancient worlds, which can only know the death of the gods, as opposed to that death of God which occurs in the Crucifixion, and which is renewed in the uniquely modern realization of the death of God. Thus it is not a pagan but a Christian Heidegger who renews the death of God in his celebration of *Ereignis*, an *Ereignis* which is a truly apocalyptic *Ereignis*, and thereby a renewal of an original Christianity, and perhaps Heidegger is nowhere more Kierkegaardian than in knowing an absolute distance between an original Christianity and all manifest or given Christianity. It is precisely his knowing this distance that makes pronunciation of the name of God impossible for Heidegger, yet that very impossibility released a profound theological thinking in Heidegger that occurs again and again in his greatest work. Even if that thinking has not yet been widely understood as a theological thinking, it can nonetheless be apprehended as theologically genuinely original. We can know that Heidegger's great philosophical predecessors were all theological thinkers, Leibnitz, Schelling, Hegel, and Nietzsche, all of them radical theological thinkers, just as is Heidegger himself. So perhaps it is his radical theological thinking that has made Heidegger so difficult to understand theologically, a radical theological thinking that is inaugurating new theological worlds.

—NOVEMBER 2001, REVISED SEPTEMBER 2009

7

MARION

Dionysian Theology as a Catholic Nihilism

Surely nothing could be more theologically audacious than an apprehension of the Crucified God by way of the mystical theology of Pseudo-Dionysius, the most purely mystical theology in the Christian tradition and also the most deeply Eastern thinking that has entered the Western world, just as it is the purest theological expression of the ancient Christian quest for mystical deification. A dialectical language is primal here, for absolute light can only be spoken and envisioned as absolute darkness, as Dionysius declares in the first part of *Mystical Theology*:

> Trinity, Super-Essential, Super-Divine, Super-Excellent! You
> Who instruct Christians in your heavenly wisdom! Guide us to
> That topmost height of mystic lore which exceeds light and
> More than exceeds knowledge, where the simple, absolute, and
> Unchangeable mysteries of heavenly truth lie hidden in the
> Dazzling obscurity of the secret Silence, outshining all
> Brilliance with the intensity of their darkness, and surcharging
> our blinded intellects with the utterly impalpable and invisible
> fairness of glories which exceed all beauty! Such be my prayer,
> and you, dear Trinity, I counsel that, in the earnest exercise of

of mystic contemplation, you leave the senses and the activities
of the intellect and all things that the senses or the intellect can
perceive, and all things in this world of nothingness, or in the
world of being, and that, your understanding being laid to rest,
you strain (so far as you may), towards a union with Him whom
neither being nor understanding can contain. For the unceasing
and absolute renunciation of yourself and all things, you will in
purity cast all things aside, and be released from all, and so will
be led upwards in the Ray of that divine Darkness which exceeds
all Existence. (Rolt translation, somewhat modified by author)

A purely mystical theology has always challenged being, or challenged any possible being that can be apprehended in the depths of
our understanding, and this is just as true of Meister Eckhart as it is of
Pseudo-Dionysius. This is the deep ground of every genuine negative
theology, and it is inseparable from the mystical goal of deification, a
deification that is the way of absolute return, so that for Eriugena, the
purest follower of Pseudo-Dionysius in the West, the final end of humanity is not simply to become one with God, but through grace "to
become God himself" (*Periphyseon*, book 5). Can such a deification be
understood as "the crossing of Being"? Is this the deeper meaning of a
Christian redemption through union with the Crucified Christ? Nothing could be a greater offense to our dominant Western Christianity,
or to the great body of our Western theology, or even to virtually all
of our Christologies. How ironic that, in *God without Being*, Jean-Luc
Marion's understanding of the "crossing of Being" is realized by way of
a renewal of Heidegger, so that Heidegger's destruction or deconstruction of the history of ontology can now seemingly issue in an epiphany
of the Crucified God, an epiphany that can only be a transcendence or
reversal of *das Sein*.

Marion's refusal of the primacy of the *one* over every other divine
name is surely in the spirit of Pseudo-Dionysius, if not in the spirit of
Eastern Orthodoxy as a whole, and if this "idol" of God is abolished by
the luminous darkness, is that the darkness wherein the Crucified God
is manifest? Marion affirms that every doctrine of divine names strives
to "destruct" (in the Heideggerian sense) the idolatrous primacy of a
human point of view, and that theology must choose either to proceed

by the apprehension of concepts, as a "science," or, if it wills to be *theo-logical*, it will choose to submit all its concepts to a "destruction" by the doctrine of the divine names. Aquinas, and perhaps the whole body of modern Catholic theology, has chosen the first way, a way that has culminated in the dissolution or death of every concept of God, and a way that can be reversed only by a full acceptance of the darkness of the crossed or crucified God. Ever since Aquinas, theological understanding has been unable to realize a properly Christian name of the God who is revealed in Jesus Christ, of that God who is *agape* for that God who gives himself as *agape*, thereby marks his divergence from Being, and must necessarily be absent from every understanding grounded in the primacy or the ultimacy of Being.

Consequently Marion calls for a liberation from Being, or rather a freedom rendered to Being, so that its own "play" can be allowed to liberate itself and above all to liberate itself from that ontological difference between Being and beings which is the deepest ground of our dominant Western ontologies. Of course, Marion speaks as though there is only one metaphysics and one metaphysical tradition, which is absurd historically, but fully understandable for one who is so profoundly rebelling against Thomism. Perhaps only from Paris could a demand now come forth calling for a return to the Bible from metaphysical scholasticism, as though this were something new in history, then proceeding to a scholastic examination of a few isolated biblical texts wholly removed from their own context and from any possible historical or critical understanding. It is as though thirteenth-century Paris were reborn in the twentieth century, albeit with deep assistance from Heidegger, but it is not to be forgotten that Heidegger was originally molded by such scholasticism. And perhaps we are witnessing a renewal of an original Parisian rejection of Aquinas, one once again occurring by way of a Christian Neoplatonism and once again calling upon the primacy of episcopal authority. Could Paris now be the primal site of the reversal of all radical thinking, a radical thinking that only recently was most powerful in Paris itself, and could this, too, be a renewal of thirteenth-century Paris, a Paris giving birth to that absolute monarchy which ruled the Western world for half a millennium? Yet it was Paris that brought that monarchy to an end in the French Revolution, thereby decisively ending the ancient world as a whole, so that perhaps in a Parisian context there can be no ultimate difference between radical and reactionary thinking.

Marion is certainly radical in calling for the "crossing" of Being, a crossing tracing a cross over all ontological difference, but a cross that abolishes it without deconstructing it, exceeds it without overcoming it, annuls it without annihilating it. Could this be a Catholic dialectical *Aufhebung*? And is this truly manifest in Marion's centering upon "the gift" as that which crosses the ontological difference of Being/being? Now Being/being is given according to the gift, a gift that delivers or redeems Being/being, and does so both by launching it into its destiny and by liberating being from Being, or liberating Being/being from ontological difference. The gift is *agape*, an *agape* that is the gift of the crossed or crucified God, or of that God who is revealed only in the disappearance of his death and resurrection. The Crucified God "gives": "The giving, in allowing to be divined how 'it gives' a giving, offers the only accessible trace of He who gives" (*God without Being*, 105). Then Marion actually employs the word *relève*, Derrida's translation of Hegel's *Aufhebung*, to speak of that only accessible trace, a trace recording neither abolition nor continuation, but rather a resumption that simultaneously surpasses and maintains. Marion immediately thereafter calls upon Pseudo-Dionysius, a thinker infinitely distant from Hegel, and thereby perhaps most distant from the ontology and the theology of Western Christianity, but a thinker rejoicing in a deeply mystical call that we become messengers announcing the divine silence.

Is "the gift" then a gift that can only be known in silence, a silence that is the silence of the divine darkness? But if we are to be messengers of that silence, does that not demand that we abandon everything whatsoever in this "world of nothingness" and in the "world of being," an abandonment apart from which there can be no epiphany for us of absolute darkness? Clearly Marion is calling us to such a silence and to such a darkness, and in this perspective, there surely could be no possible "continuation," no possible continuity between the false light of our world and the absolute darkness of the Godhead. Here, annulment clearly is annihilation, but in the deeper traditions of negative theology that annihilation is simply the reverse side of deification, and we can only realize the divine darkness by being truly and fully united with that darkness. And that is precisely why the absolute light of the Godhead can only be absolute darkness to us, only in a human perspective is that light manifest as light, or only insofar as it is comprehended as either Being or being. Now there can be no doubt that Aquinas himself profoundly wrestled with Pseudo-Dionysius, again and again in the

Summa Theologica incorporating the writing of Dionysius into his own, and perhaps Dionysius was the thinker who most challenged Aquinas, even as it was Spinoza who most challenged Hegel. And just as Hegel could know Spinoza as the purest pantheist in the history of Western thinking, we can know Pseudo-Dionysius as the purest pantheist in the history of Christian thinking, and a pantheist who even created a Catholic pantheism, wherein the Hierarchy of the Church is conjoined with an Angelic Hierarchy, so as to witness to if not to embody a Catholic Church that is all in all. Such a theological totalitarianism profoundly fascinated the medieval mind, and there are many who understand the great victory of Aquinas as a victory over such a mystical totality, a victory making possible a whole new thinking and a whole new civilization, and a civilization that could not only know but could fully act within and upon the actuality of the world as world.

Yet Marion knows Aquinas as the enactor of the greatest fall in the history of theology, a fall wherein the God revealed in Jesus Christ is summoned to enter the role of the divine in metaphysics, in assuming *esse/ens* as his proper name (82). More neutrally, one could speak of Aquinas as the creator of a Christian Aristotelian metaphysics, one that was deeply opposed by Augustinian Neoplatonic theologians, and the Parisian condemnation of 1277 was certainly directed against Thomistic propositions, and the main thrust of the Parisian condemnation was to preserve the omnipotence of God by His "absolute power" (Weisheipl, *Friar Thomas D'Aquino*, 339). It was an Aristotelian potentiality and actuality that most offended these theologians, who believed that this was a sacrifice of the absolute power of the Creator, and accordingly a capitulation to a pagan bondage to the power of the world. Just as Marion can understand the theology of Aquinas as a capitulation issuing in the death of the metaphysical God, Aquinas' contemporary Neoplatonic opponents could understand Thomism in much the same manner, even as modern Eastern Orthodox Christians such as Dostoevsky can respond to Roman Catholicism itself as the very source of atheism. Indeed, such an ultimate protest has long been present in France, and most forcefully and openly in a radical Jansenism, which is perhaps being reborn in Marion today.

Now if a pure nihilism can only theologically be manifest as a pure atheism, is a pure reaction against that atheism inevitably a nihilistic reaction, and nihilistic in the very violence of its assault upon all manifest actuality? Certainly modern nihilism is atheistic, and if this is a nihilism

that is a consequence of modernity itself, it is a consequence of an atheistic modernity, as was deeply known by Nietzsche himself. Yet a religious totality can evolve a genuine nihilism, as manifest in Gnosticism,
and Hans Jonas, who perhaps understood Gnosticism most deeply in
our world, could understand it as a violent reaction against the classical world, and could even do so in the perspective of his own revulsion
against a Nazi nihilism, a nihilism that was a barbarous counterrevolution against civilization itself. Yet Nietzsche understood Christianity
and the Christian God as the ultimate origin of our nihilism, or the
origin of an absolute No-saying, a No-saying manifest in the revulsion
of patristic Christianity against the classical world, a Christianity which
was arguably the origin of ancient Gnosticism. Now even if Plotinus
was the deepest opponent of Gnosticism in the ancient world, that
Christian Neoplatonism inspired by Plotinus evolved ever more fully
into an absolute otherworldliness fully parallel to Gnosticism, as manifest so purely in Pseudo-Dionysius.

This is the Neoplatonism that is most totally assaulted by Nietzsche, yet the young Nietzsche was deeply tempted by its modern counterpart, which he could name as the Dionysian. *The Birth of Tragedy*
knows Dionysian ecstasy as a dismemberment of everything that has
been experienced by the individual, as individuation itself is here identified as the source of all suffering and all evil. Modernity, above all in
Hegel and Nietzsche, can know an individual consciousness as being
born in ancient Greece, and both Hegel and Nietzsche could know
the Greek mystery cults as effecting reversals of this new individual
consciousness, mystery cults that are reborn in the advent of Christianity. But it is in full Christian Neoplatonism that this reversal is
most total, and certainly in Pseudo-Dionysius, who gives us a Christian Dionysianism which is a dismemberment of consciousness itself,
a dismemberment so radical that everything other than the Godhead
is actually manifest as an absolute nothingness. Indeed, it is only by
knowing everything as an absolute nothingness that we can actually
know the Godhead, a Godhead who can only be manifest to us as an
absolute darkness, and a darkness bringing to an end every possible
source of light.

Is this not a genuine nihilism? And is it providence itself that
conferred the Christian name of Dionysius, a Dionysius who is truly
the opposite of the Greek Dionysus, yet if the Greek Dionysus is the
mystery god par excellence, is a Christian Dionysianism the purest

mysticism, a mysticism that is a total deification? Here, total deification is a total return to Godhead itself, a return only possible by way
of returning from everything that has evolved in consciousness and history, so that a Catholic Dionysianism is an absolute dissolution and
reversal of history and consciousness. Is a new Catholic Dionysianism
at hand in our world, one made possible by the collapse of all Catholic
scholasticisms and the dismemberment of a uniquely modern Catholic
tradition, one now being effected by the Catholic hierarchy? Is Marion
a spokesman for a truly new Catholic theology, one far more Dionysian
than Catholic theology has ever been before, one impossible for Western Christianity until the advent of a truly new world? And is it the advent of a truly new and even absolute nihilism that can make possible
the realization of a new Catholic Dionysianism, a nihilism realizing the
nothingness of everything whatsoever, thereby perhaps calling forth an
absolute return to the Godhead only by way of realizing the nothingness of all and everything?

That Dionysian theology that Marion calls forth is not a renewal
but far rather a resurrection of Catholicism; resurrection is from the
dead, and absolute resurrection is resurrection from absolute death, an
absolute death occurring in an absolute nihilism, but a nihilism essential to this resurrection of Catholicism. Not until all and everything is
truly known as nothingness itself can Catholicism be genuinely resurrected, a resurrection that is an absolute return to the Godhead and precisely thereby an absolute deification. A purer Catholicism has always
known redemption as deification, and absolute redemption as absolute
deification, and if modern Catholicism has moved away from deification, that has been a Catholicism in crisis if only because of our comprehensive nihilism. But this Catholicism's ending could make possible
the realization of a truly Dionysian Catholicism. Modern Catholicism
has always been in deep opposition to modernity, and perhaps most so
in France where counterrevolution has been most powerful, a counterrevolution called forth by the French Revolution, making impossible
all modern theology in France. All too significantly a new and total
Neoplatonism is most powerful in France, and if this is giving birth
to a new Dionysian theology, that theology is impossible apart from a
counterrevolution against nihilism, which is perhaps what a new Dionysian theology actually is.

—OCTOBER 1993, REVISED AUGUST 2009

8

Contemporary French Thinking and the Primordial

At a time when the most advanced French thinking is apparently renewing if not creating a move to the absolutely primordial, even to an absolutely primordial Godhead, as in Levinas, Derrida, and Marion, we should become open to another and contrary French tradition, one embodying an ultimate move from God the Creator to the Crucified God. If genuine modern thinking begins with radical doubt, this is present not only in Descartes but also in Pascal, as here a radical doubt is directed against modernity itself, thereby realizing an ultimate chasm between God and the world. Pascal can be understood as the polar opposite of Descartes, and if God hides himself for each of these thinkers, that hiddenness is far more profound in Pascal than in Descartes, as for Pascal everything whatsoever bears the mark of this hiddenness. This issues in a radical Pascalian move from God the Creator to God the Suffering Savior, a move embodied in that radical Jansenism which can be understood as the deepest religious underground of France, one occurring again and again in France's greatest modern writers, and which has been apprehended as a primal ground of the French Revolution itself. That revolution in turn called forth the greatest counterrevolution in history, and the French Church then became and perhaps remains even today the most conservative or reactionary of all religious bodies, so that radical theology is rarer in France than in any other advanced country.

A move to the absolutely primordial can be understood as an ultimately conservative or reactionary move, hence it might be expected
that this would occur in contemporary France, but France has also
been a site of ultimate and even absolute revolution, not only in politics but also in the imaginative realm. Is this not possible in French
theological thinking, or is it in fact occurring, even if unknown to the
world at large? The contemporary French religious thinker who has had
the greatest impact beyond France is Simone Weil, who is clearly in the
Pascalian or Jansenist tradition, although she profoundly radicalizes it,
for here not only does the Crucified God become all in all, but the Creator himself passes into the Crucified God and does so in the self-emptying act of the creation. While this could be apprehended as a deeply
Hegelian movement, Hegel himself was closed to its ultimate religious
and political consequences, and if a renewal of Hegelian thinking gave
birth to radical French thinking during the Second World War and its
aftermath, that thinking is least radical in the theological realm, where
it is profoundly conservative or reactionary. Is there a deeper or purer
image of God as absolute Creator and Judge than Lacan's Phallus? Here
a new and comprehensive *horror religiosus* is reborn, and as opposed to
Hegel's abstract Spirit or Bad Infinite, which themselves are the consequence of an absolute self-negation or self-emptying of Absolute Spirit,
these contemporary evocations are absolutely primordial, evoking that
absolutely primordial which is absolute ground and source.

Such evocations are wholly opposed to any possible self-negation
or self-emptying, but so too is the Infinite of Levinas, as well as that
radically Neoplatonic One which is so hypnotizing the French mind
today. Yet dialectically these movements could be understood as integrally and essentially related to their very opposites, and as themselves
impossible apart from the full realization of those opposites; for if contemporary French thinkers have given us our most awesome evocations
of God the Creator, is that possible apart from an absolute negation and
reversal of that which is the very opposite of such a Creator? Of course,
this ultimate negation was created by Hegel, and is the deepest ground
of Hegelian thinking, but Hegelian thinking moves in a truly opposite
direction, for it is a forward movement to absolute apocalypse rather
than a backward movement to the absolutely primordial. Kierkegaard
could know such a backward movement as the pagan movement of
recollection as opposed to the biblical movement of forward-moving
repetition, a repetition that is inseparable from an absolute negation

of the archaic movement of eternal return. Nowhere in our world has the archaic movement of eternal return been more deeply reborn than in contemporary French thinking, but is this only possible by way of the negation and reversal of its opposite, and could this therefore be evidence of the deep even if underground presence of that opposite in France and the world itself today?

In an American perspective, the absolutely primordial is inseparable from Melville's epic vision of the White Whale, and if that vision is a uniquely American enactment of the death of God, here the White Whale is an incarnate *horror religiosus*, as the only possible primordial here is an absolutely dark and chaotic primordial. But is it possible to apprehend any other mode or epiphany of the primordial today, and if a deeper encounter with a Lacan or a Derrida inevitably induces an ultimate tremor or *Angst*, an *Angst* that is the consequence of an encounter with the Nothing, is a uniquely contemporary primordial inseparable from that Nothing? Sartre is the one French thinker who dared fully to think about the Nothing, but the Nothing is being called forth in contemporary Neoplatonic thinking, our most openly primordial thinking. Although Heidegger is our greatest primordial thinker since Plotinus he nevertheless radically restricted his explicit thinking about the Nothing. Certainly radical contemporary French thinking would have been impossible apart from both Hegel and Heidegger, and if Hegel is an openly theological thinker and Heidegger a cryptic one, must primordial thinking now be cryptic or elusive precisely because of its inseparability from an absolute nothingness?

Although Hegel was the first philosopher to think fully about an absolute nothingness, which is a primal center of the *Science of Logic*, he thinks that nothingness only to negate it absolutely, and if this is possible for an apocalyptic thinker, is it impossible for a primordial thinker? Apparently Heidegger was never able to realize such a negation or even to attempt it; is such a negation then impossible within a primordial horizon, or impossible apart from an absolute darkening or absolute emptying of the primordial itself? Certainly such an emptying occurs in a purely Hegelian thinking, but that thinking is only possible by way of an actual realization of the death of God, a death that is a self-negation or a self-emptying of an absolute transcendence, and a death that can be understood theologically as a conceptual realization of the Crucified God. But that conceptual realization is simultaneously a historical realization, one only possible within a Christian horizon and furthermore only possible within the horizon of the full and actual advent of the third and final Age of the Spirit. Just as Hegel is our first apocalyptic philosopher, he is the first philosopher fully to integrate historical and conceptual thinking, and here Heidegger himself is a Hegelian thinker and all too significantly an apocalyptic as well as a primordial thinker who more than any other contemporary thinker continually called forth the apocalyptic crisis of our world, a crisis inseparable from the redemptive advent of an apocalyptic *Ereignis*.

Yet such an *Ereignis* is wholly missing from primordial thinking today; perhaps no other word is more untranslatable in any contemporary language. This is a situation that can be understood as reflecting a uniquely contemporary theological crisis, a crisis in which it is impossible to think God and apocalypse at once. This is true of Heidegger too, for even if Heidegger refused to think God, he never ceased being a theological thinker, and just as Heidegger could understand the death of God as an ontotheological event, it is an event inseparable from the apocalyptic advent of *Ereignis*. Hence that advent is truly inseparable from what the Christian knows as the Crucified God, and just as Heidegger was profoundly affected by Paul as early as his 1920 lectures on the phenomenology of religion, it is the authentic Pauline epistles that center upon the Crucifixion, and here the Crucifixion is apocalypse itself. Although in 1920 Heidegger could know the apocalyptic Paul already, in advance of New Testament scholarship, theology even today has yet to realize the Crucifixion as apocalypse, despite both Paul and the Fourth Gospel. Is it simply impossible today to think God and apocalypse at once, or impossible now to think the Crucified God, to understand the Crucified God as the self-embodiment of an actual and apocalyptic death of Godhead itself?

At no point is Hegel's thinking more ambivalent than at this crucial point, and if Nietzsche went beyond Hegel in his enactment of the death of God, Nietzsche is a more purely apocalyptic thinker than is Hegel, perhaps because he could know the apocalyptic finality of the death of God. There can be little doubt that the God whom Nietzsche knew to be dead is the uniquely Christian God, but this God who is known in Christianity is a consequence of a radical de-eschatologizing of the original Christian kerygma, or an ultimate transformation of an original apocalyptic Christianity into Hellenistic Christianity, one entailing not only a profound transformation of Jesus, but a transformation of the apocalyptic Kingdom of God that Jesus enacted and embodied into an absolutely sovereign and absolutely transcendent God. Jesus proclaimed that Kingdom of God which is dawning even now, though it will only be consummated in the future, and the actualization of this "kingdom" is a truly forward-moving one, one moving toward an absolute and final apocalypse. Historical Christianity, however, or the great body of historical Christianity, has known God as the absolutely primordial Creator, and the way to this God is a backward way to the absolutely primordial. Indeed, it is only after the advent of Christianity that Godhead itself is manifest in the West, an absolutely primordial Godhead, and if this is most clearly manifest in Neoplatonism, all ancient Christian thinkers were Neoplatonic thinkers, but as opposed to the purely Neoplatonic One, an absolutely indeterminate and undifferentiated One, the Christian God is absolutely primordial or absolutely "first."

This is clearest in the orthodox Christian doctrine of the Trinity, for the Father or Creator is the only person of the Godhead who is "unoriginate," and the Creator or the first person of the Trinity eternally generates the Son and the Spirit; this is the ultimate ground of the real distinctions between the persons of the Godhead. If only thereby the Christian doctrine of the Trinity is truly unique. Not only is a Christian Godhead truly unique, but it is so in its absolute transcendence, as above all manifest in the Creator, who is the begetter of the Son and the Spirit, thus giving the Creator an absolute transcendence that cannot be discovered in pure Neoplatonism, and is likewise unknown in Hindu and Buddhist trinitarianism, to say nothing of Judaism and Islam. Yet this uniquely Christian transcendence is vastly distant from that Kingdom of God which Jesus enacted and proclaimed, a Kingdom whose movement is from transcendence to immanence, or from the beyond to the here and now, and a Kingdom that Paul could know as even now becoming all in all. So it is that a uniquely Christian Creator is absent from the New Testament itself, and is only possible as a de-eschatologizing of the New Testament. If this was the greatest or the purest transformation which ever historically occurred, this very transformation is inseparable from the epiphany or the realization of the uniquely Christian God.

Whitehead, the one major twentieth-century philosopher who could actually think God, knew the uniquely Christian God as Caesar reborn, as Christian orthodoxy only fully realized itself while Christianity was undergoing an ultimate transformation into an imperial religion, and if as a result Church and State are truly united, this occurs in the first truly totalitarian imperium, for it is the first to realize an imperium that is internal and external at once. Christian orthodoxy was finally realized in that imperium, an orthodoxy even more rigid and total in the Christian West than in the Christian East, such that, as noted earlier in chapter 6, Heidegger could know "Latinization" as the transformation of a uniquely Greek truth or *aletheia* into a Roman imperium, wherein the domination of command passes into the very essence of ecclesiastical dogma (*Parmenides* §3). This is a dogma that is centered in the Trinity, and just as the dogma of the Trinity is the most orthodox of all dogmas, it is that dogma which is most resistant to an interior, or imaginative, or conceptual appropriation. While Augustine does realize an interior and conceptual appropriation of the Trinity in *De Trinitate*, this is a unique theological text, and all too significantly a pure and full thinking of the Trinity does not occur until Hegel, when it occurs only by way of the most profoundly heterodox thinking that had yet been realized, and then only by way of a pure thinking of the absolute self-negation or self-emptying of God.

Nothing could be further from ancient Christian thinking than an absolute self-emptying or self-negation, but so too is that thinking alienated from any possibility of apocalypse, or alienated from any apocalypse which is not a realization of a primordial totality, so that in orthodox Christianity apocalypse is at bottom a consequence of an absolute and eternal return. Nowhere else in the world does a purely backward movement more predominate, for Eastern visions of totality eschew every possible image of forward or backward, or every possible distinction between alpha and omega; only in Christianity is a purely backward movement possible, and an absolutely backward movement to a truly primordial totality. This is the very Christianity that is the consequence of a reversal of a purely apocalyptic movement, as only the reversal of a purely forward movement makes possible a purely backward movement, so that this backward movement is truly unique to Christianity. What modernity knows as regression is only possible within a Christian horizon, just as what Nietzsche knows as *ressentiment* is a uniquely Christian *ressentiment*. And just as no historical world has known guilt more totally than has Christianity, it is Christianity and Christianity alone that knows what Nietzsche understood as the "bad conscience." In this perspective, Kafka can be understood ironically as a Christian visionary, and even Levinas can be apprehended as having a Christian ground, and just as Nietzsche knows this guilt most profoundly, it is Nietzsche who most fully calls for its absolute reversal.

Yet that reversal for Nietzsche is an absolute Yes-saying that is an absolute apocalypse, a Yes-saying possible only by way of the reversal of an absolute No-saying, that No-saying which is Nietzsche's purest symbol of the uniquely Christian God. Thus a Christian apocalypse is uniquely Christian, for it can be discovered within no other historical horizon, and is only possible by way of what Nietzsche knows as the death of God. Of course, this is true for Hegel too, who enacts a radical movement from God the Creator to the Crucified God, wherein Crucifixion alone makes apocalypse possible, an apocalypse that is an absolute reversal of sovereignty and transcendence, and thus the realization of an absolutely kenotic or absolutely self-emptying immanence. Though Hegel and Nietzsche may have realized this movement most profoundly in the modern world, was this movement inaugurated in France, and even historically embodied in a radical Jansenism, so that when contemporary French philosophy was reborn in our world through an absorption of Hegel and Nietzsche, was that movement in continuity with a radical French tradition? Is it possible that the rebirth of primordial thinking in France today embodies a demand to reverse that tradition, and if the very purity of such primordial thinking is now unique to France, is that inseparable from a uniquely French kenotic tradition? Is there now the possibility of a rebirth of that kenotic tradition, or is such a rebirth already occurring in a radical French theology? If so, let it be manifest to the world at large!

—FEBRUARY 2003, REVISED 2010

9

MODERNITY AND THE ORIGIN OF *ANGST*

While *Angst* is a distinctively if not uniquely modern category, and most so insofar as it is known as a consequence of an encounter with the Nothing, it nonetheless purports to call forth a universal human condition, even if one only possible by way of an ultimate crisis. Kierkegaard and Heidegger are our deepest thinkers of *Angst*, as both think *Angst* by way of thinking the Nothing, yet neither engaged in a full or decisive thinking of the Nothing. Indeed, even if this is perhaps the primal question of Eastern philosophy, the only Western philosophers who are profoundly engaged with the question of the Nothing are Schelling, Hegel, Nietzsche, and Heidegger. For the great body of our philosophy is closed to the question of the Nothing, although nothing is more primal in truly modern or late modern poetry than is the Nothing itself, a Nothing finally eliciting an ultimate celebration, as most openly occurring in Mallarmé and Stevens.

Now it is not insignificant that Kierkegaard and Heidegger, our deepest thinkers of *Angst*, are precisely thereby our deepest modern thinkers of guilt, and a guilt which each knew as being uniquely Christian, and thereby inseparable from a uniquely Christian grace, and uniquely Christian in being dialectically inseparable from sin, a dialectic discovered by Paul and fully formulated theologically by Augustine. An original forgiveness of sin is necessarily and inevitably a realization of the most ultimate guilt, one unmanifest and inactual until this forgiveness, but one now actualized to make possible an ultimate forgiveness. Such ultimate forgiveness or absolute gift is only possible through the absolute transfiguration of its very opposite, and an absolute transfiguration impossible apart from the actual realization of that opposite. So it is that Christianity can know the deepest grace only by knowing the deepest guilt, a guilt which is itself a decisive sign of that grace, as so profoundly reflected in Augustine implicitly and in Luther and Kierkegaard explicitly, and both Augustine and Luther created historical revolutions by way of this realization. This guilt, known as an actual nothingness, is not fully realized in thinking until the advent of German Idealism, an idealism first giving us in Schelling and Hegel an actual understanding of the Nothing, or that Nothing which is an actual Nothing, and an actual Nothing only possible by way of an original forgiveness of sin or an original absolute Gift.

That German "idealism" is a truly new philosophical realism, the first philosophy to become open to history itself and to the imagination, and the first to become open to the depths of evil, an opening inseparable from its realization of an actual nothingness. If Hegel and Nietzsche are purely dialectical thinkers, Heidegger is profoundly under their impact, and thus at least implicitly dialectical. Thus in *Being and Time* the very understanding of *Angst* and death is inseparable from an ultimate call, just as in *Beiträge* the understanding of *Ereignis* is the calling forth of an absolute advent which is an absolute ending, an eschatological ending that is apocalypse itself. We are now coming to realize that Schelling, Hegel, Nietzsche, Heidegger, and Wittgenstein are the most theological of our modern philosophers, and also those very philosophers who have given us our deepest understanding of the Nothing. Here the Nothing is inseparable from an absolute uprooting or an absolute disruption, a rupture bringing an end to every possible calm, every possible quiescence, thus realizing the advent of actuality itself, a wholly negative actuality that only now is all in all.

This is the actuality that we are called on to accept as an ultimate gift, but it is a gift inseparable from death and fallenness, once again calling forth a uniquely Christian *felix culpa*, a fortunate fall that is grace itself, and a grace inseparable from an ultimate *Angst*. Now if it is the Incarnation which Christian thinkers commonly understand as the absolute paradox, in this perspective that paradox can be known as a universal paradox, a paradox manifest in every actual opening to either sin or grace, and every actual opening to actuality itself. Already

Paul deeply knows this, and knows it in experiencing the advent of an absolute grace that is inseparable from the advent of an absolute guilt, so if it is Paul who is the source of what Nietzsche so profoundly knows as the "bad conscience," he is even thereby the original unveiler of what we have most deeply known as grace, an unveiling inseparable from the unveiling of an absolute guilt. Many of our most creative contemporary philosophers are now being profoundly challenged by Paul, and if Nietzsche is our most deeply Pauline late modern thinker, he can be so only by way of the mirage of being a pure enemy of Paul, an enemy releasing *The Anti-Christ*, which many now regard as his greatest work. Of course, it was Paul who made possible the Augustinian revolution, a revolution inaugurating a uniquely Western dialectical thinking, so that a Western dialectical thinking can be understood as a genuinely Pauline thinking, and this is just as true of Hegel's thinking as it is of Kierkegaard's and Nietzsche's.

Now if a fully actual nothingness only becomes historically incarnate with the advent of Christianity, this advent is inseparable from the forgiveness of sin, an apocalyptic forgiveness of sin occurring in the depths of "darkness," and one therein calling forth those very depths, depths invisible and unheard apart from such an apocalyptic forgiveness, but depths now speakable and hearable as darkness itself, or as a full and actual nothingness. Just as Hegel in the conclusion of the *Science of Logic* could understand the "cunning of reason" as the reversal of every actual intention and goal, so the advent of an actual nothingness can be understood as a reversal of the apparent goal of forgiveness; it is nonetheless a reversal necessary for an absolute or apocalyptic forgiveness, and necessary if only to actualize that absolute guilt or absolute darkness which is negated in an absolute forgiveness. But what is that negation? It certainly cannot be a dissolution of guilt or darkness, if only because the reverberations of that negation are historically so overwhelming, reverberations inaugurating an absolute guilt and a fully actual nothingness.

Thus an apocalyptic forgiveness of sin cannot be understood as a dissolution of sin but far rather as the transfiguration of sin, a transfiguration realizing an absolute reversal of sin, a reversal in which the depths of sin are reversed into the depths of grace, thus creating an absolutely new grace that is only manifest and actual as such upon the horizon of a total darkness. Accordingly, the New Testament is unique in scripture in calling forth a total guilt and a total darkness—at no other point does it so clearly differ from the Hebrew scriptures or from world scripture—but such darkness is a necessary horizon for a witness to or calling forth of total forgiveness or total grace, and if that grace is apocalypse itself, a genuine apocalypse is absolute light and absolute darkness at once and simultaneously. This is a simultaneity that can be discovered not only in the epic enactments of Dante, Milton, Blake, and Joyce, but in Nietzsche's enactment of Eternal Recurrence and Heidegger's celebration of *Ereignis*, all of which can be understood as consequences of the advent of an actual nothingness, or of an absolute transfiguration realized only in and by that advent. Hence an *Angst* arising from an encounter with the Nothing is only made possible by an apocalyptic forgiveness realizing the horizon of an actual nothingness, a horizon apart from which the Nothing would be wholly inactual and unreal, but within which the Nothing is inevitably manifest, or manifest to those who are truly awake.

Luther, Kierkegaard, and Heidegger can all know *Angst* as effecting the deepest possible call or summons to us; this is a call only possible as a consequence of the advent of a full and actual Nothing, a nothingness actualized by that forgiveness of sin which is an absolute transfiguration. Only now does darkness itself become incarnate, which can be understood as a consequence of that Incarnation which culminates in the Descent into Hell, a Descent into Hell which is a Harrowing of Hell, a harrowing that is not only virtually absent in Christian theology, but in Christian imagery and iconography as well. Why such a profound silence? Indeed, the New Testament itself is almost silent on this crucial front, and this despite the fact that the New Testament is more centered upon damnation and Hell than any other scripture in the world. Nevertheless, Paul could deeply affirm in the context of his purest apocalyptic writing that for our sake God made Christ who knew no sin "to be sin" (2 Cor. 5:21), but this statement is unique in the New Testament and has apparently never called forth an actual Christian imagery. Yet such an affirmation is clearly a dialectical one, and if Paul is the creator of a uniquely Christian dialectic, and is so by inaugurating the apprehension of a true dialectical movement in which opposites actually pass into each other, so that the depths of sin pass into the depths of grace, even as the depths of grace pass into the depths of sin, then we can understand not only that the opposites of sin and grace are actually inseparable, but that their very full and final actualization embodies an ultimate *coincidentia oppositorum*.

Here, too, lies a uniquely Western and Christian *coincidentia oppositorum*, realizing interior depths that are truly dichotomous depths, wherein an ultimate transfiguration can occur, and a transfiguration of the ultimate depths of evil itself. No such transfiguration can occur apart from the realization of the depths of nothingness, therein making possible the advent of what a deeper imagination and a deeper thinking can know as the Nothing, yet a Nothing which is the very opposite of a simple or pure nothingness, and is so by way of its own ultimate actuality. A Christian naming of the Nothing occurs in a Christian naming of Satan, but at no point is our theology weaker and more fragmentary than it is in its understanding of Satan, nor at any other point does it stand so wholly removed from our imaginative creations, imaginative creations which in full and late modernity call forth ultimate enactments of Satan and Hell. Even as this occurs in epic vision, theology ever more fully removes itself from any possible understanding of Satan and Hell, muting itself also on the subject of damnation, which is truly central in all premodern theology, thus giving us a theology that is wholly closed to absolute transfiguration, and is so if only because it is alienated from the depths of evil and darkness.

Of course, there is little understanding of evil in our philosophical traditions, as an in-depth philosophical understanding of evil does not occur until German Idealism, and then disappears in twentieth-century philosophy, despite the profound and overwhelming enactments of evil in the late modern imagination. Now we cannot say that it is impossible to think the depths of evil if only because this so fully occurs in Schelling, Hegel, and Nietzsche, and if these are the very thinkers who embody the depths of the imagination, that is a depth inseparable from the depths of evil, depths of evil making possible that absolute transfiguration occurring throughout our greatest imaginative creations. It is a philosophical understanding of that transfiguration that makes German Idealism possible, as most purely and comprehensively occurring in Hegel's dialectical philosophy of absolute negation, an absolute negation that is absolute transfiguration, and absolute transfiguration of absolute opposites. While it is Nietzsche who most ultimately inverts and reverses this dialectical negation, despite having little acquaintance with Hegel, this is an absolute inversion which is nonetheless an absolute dialectical negation, as an absolute No-saying passes into an absolute Yes-saying, a Yes-saying wholly impossible apart from that No-saying.

Nietzsche's enactment of Eternal Recurrence is an enactment of absolute transfiguration, a transfiguration impossible apart from calling forth the depths of abyss and darkness, depths which are themselves transfigured in this enactment, as here the deepest darkness passes into the deepest light, or absolute No is transfigured into absolute Yes. While Nietzsche apparently stands alone as the philosopher of Eternal Recurrence, the truth is that Eternal Recurrence fully parallels a uniquely modern dialectical negation, so that Hegel and Nietzsche can be understood as dialectical twins, for if each is the very opposite of the other, these are opposites that nonetheless coincide, and do so as purely dialectical thinkers. Only Heidegger has fully conjoined these thinkers, and done so as a thinker who is simultaneously ontological and historical at once, and simultaneously systematic and anti-systematic at once, thereby conjoining our greatest modern systematic thinker and the greatest anti-systematic thinker who ever lived. So, too, Heidegger is a deeply theological and deeply anti-theological thinker at once, thereby once again conjoining Hegel and Nietzsche, and if all three of these thinkers profoundly know the death of God, each of them can finally realize that death as an ultimate liberation.

This is the liberation that dawns as the forgiveness of sin, and the apocalyptic forgiveness of sin, and if that forgiveness is inseparable from an enactment of the deepest depths of darkness, depths called forth by that very forgiveness, a philosophy of absolute transfiguration transfigures these very depths, and this occurs in the deeper thinking of Hegel and Nietzsche and Heidegger alike. So, too, does it occur in our deepest imaginative vision, one realized philosophically by Schelling and Hegel, and by Nietzsche and Heidegger, too, and these are our only philosophers who embody imaginative vision. Yet transfiguration is ultimately and at bottom a theological rather than philosophical category; it does not occur in our philosophical dictionaries, perhaps because it is inseparable from a theological or ultimate redemption, a redemption from the depths of evil and abyss. Dialectical philosophy has itself perished in the twentieth century, or perished except where it is embodied in Marxism, but Marxism has given us our deepest and most comprehensive understanding of evil in the twentieth century, and if Marxist enactments of redemption are truly reversed in that century, nothing else has so darkened the very idea or symbol of redemption.

Now not only does Nietzsche fully and ecstatically employ a language of redemption, but this occurs at least partially in Heidegger as well, and explicitly so whenever he speaks of *Ereignis*. This occurs far more decisively in these thinkers than it does in our modern theologians, at least apart from that solitary genius Karl Barth. Perhaps no language has been so emptied in modernity as has theological language, an inevitable consequence of a uniquely modern realization of the death of God, so that its occurrence in our philosophical thinkers is far more powerful than it is in virtually all of our theology, but the question must inevitably be asked if this is a genuine language of redemption. Here, Hegel has inevitably drawn the deepest assault, but that assault should necessarily be directed at Nietzsche too. Remarkably, there is a deep resistance to such assault, and perhaps it is impossible to assault Nietzsche deeply, or to annul or dissolve his language. If so, this bespeaks a truly miraculous power, one obviously absent in Schelling and Hegel, and it gives us an insight as to why Heidegger was impelled to create the densest and most difficult of all philosophical languages.

The late Nietzsche was much given to unveiling that absolute reversal which Christianity effected upon Jesus; thereby Nietzsche comes to know a Jesus whose praxis is wholly centered upon forgiveness, a forgiveness which he silently or indirectly knows as the initial enactment of the death of God, or the death of the absolute Creator and Judge. Indeed, in *The Anti-Christ* (§33) Nietzsche can proclaim that in true Christianity, the one practiced by Jesus alone, sin is abolished, and precisely this is the "glad tidings," for blessedness is not promised, it is the only reality. This is the blessedness discovered once again by Zarathustra, a new Zarathustra who enacts blessedness as Eternal Recurrence, a blessedness whose only portal is an absolute horror, the absolute horror of actuality itself. This is the horror that is ultimately blessed by an enactment of Eternal Recurrence, and just as no one has known a *horror religiosus* more deeply than has Nietzsche, this is a horror that first comes to an end through the forgiveness of Jesus, even if it is in Paul that this horror is first purely spoken. If Nietzsche and Blake are commonly known as our greatest modern prophets, at no point are they so fully united as in their ultimate enactment of an absolute forgiveness, a forgiveness only occurring through what Nietzsche knows as the death of God and Blake envisions as the "Self-Annihilation" of God, a death releasing what Nietzsche knows as an ultimate nihilism and Blake envisions as a total embodiment of Satan.

But that embodiment of Satan is so only as a "Self-Annihilation" of Satan, just as that ultimate nihilism is one reversed in Eternal

Recurrence, a reversal only possible through that nihilism itself, just as the "Self-Annihilation" of Satan is possible only through the total embodiment of Satan. For Blake and Nietzsche are those prophets who most ultimately envision and enact an absolute darkness, an enactment inseparable from either Eternal Recurrence or Self-Annihilation, and thus inseparable from everything which here can be known as an absolute forgiveness. It is remarkable how primal Jesus is both to the late Nietzsche and to the mature Blake, and both most deeply associate the name of Jesus with an absolute forgiveness, an absolute forgiveness wholly reversed by Christianity and our history itself. So, too, Blake and Nietzsche are our most offensive prophets, enacting what our common experience and common sense can know as pure blasphemies and pure assaults upon our most deeply cherished assurances and beliefs.

Is it possible today to speak of any kind of ultimate advent or ultimate beginning? Perhaps at no other point are we so distant from Hegel and Nietzsche, or so distant from a genuine historical consciousness, or from that genealogy which is so important for Nietzsche. Indeed, Nietzsche created everything that we most deeply know as genealogy, a genealogy that is a dialectical genealogy, and dialectical in knowing a genuine or ultimate origin as being the very opposite of all apparent or manifest origin. Hence it is quite Nietzschean to know the advent of *Angst* as being the consequence of an absolute forgiveness, or to know the origin of an absolute forgiveness itself as being inseparable from an ultimate curse. No one has known curse itself as purely as did Nietzsche, a curse that he could know as universal, one occurring throughout all history and consciousness and one whose origin is an original fall. It is truly remarkable that Nietzsche has known an original fall more deeply than any theologian, including even Augustine, and it is that fall that he enacts in creating an ultimate genealogy, one that is nowhere thought more deeply that it is in *On the Genealogy of Morals*.

Augustine himself can appear as an innocent in this Nietzschean perspective, a perspective profoundly reversing everything that we have known as ethics, and doing so precisely in calling forth the origin of that ethics. Here it becomes fully understandable why we would deeply resist the question of origin, a question only now becoming an absolutely forbidden question, and forbidden because, when origin becomes deeply investigated, it calls forth a true horror or a pure assault. Are our most deeply cherished ideals the very opposite of their manifest meaning, and do we inevitably come to know this when we realize a genuine genealogy, a genealogy not created until Nietzsche, but one thereafter having an overwhelming effect, and not least so through psychoanalysis? Nowhere is such a pure *dysangel* or such overwhelming "bad news" more deeply embodied than in Nietzsche, and yet no thinker has been more liberating than Nietzsche, and most liberating to those most overwhelmed by *Angst*. The very category of fall, and of ultimate fall, opens up a new perspective on *Angst*, for if *Angst* is a consequence of fall, then in a Christian context it can be known as a *felix culpa* or fortunate fall, a fall realizing that very consciousness that is transfigured in an absolute forgiveness or absolute redemption, a redemption and forgiveness impossible apart from ultimate fall.

In the deeper expressions of Western imagination, and of Western thinking too, an enactment of ultimate transfiguration is inseparable from an enactment of ultimate fall. This is perhaps clearest in Hegel, Marx, and Nietzsche, but most overwhelming in Dante, Milton, Blake, and Joyce. Yet it is Nietzsche who most decisively and most comprehensively thinks the fall, a thinking apart from which a total Yes-saying would be simply impossible. Hence any liberation that is here promised is inseparable from ultimate fall, as only an awakening to the depths of fall makes true liberation possible, so that this awakening is essential to genuine liberation. So likewise, it is essential to know ultimate fall as an original fall, a fall only possible as an original fall, for only if it is an original fall can it actually be reversed, as liberation is possible only from an original and not from an eternal fall. It is only an original and not an eternal fall that we ourselves can enact, can be responsible for, a responsibility that we accept in knowing an ultimate guilt, and apart from that guilt there can be no ultimate transfiguration.

There is a deep Western tradition centering upon absolute guilt, one initiated by Paul, then profoundly carried forward by Augustine, Luther, Kierkegaard, Nietzsche, and Heidegger, but this is simultaneously a tradition centering upon an ultimate liberation, and not only a liberation from that guilt but a liberation transfiguring that guilt. This transfiguration is possible only if guilt is an actual guilt, and an actual guilt that is a truly actual nothingness, a nothingness that is not a privation of being but a full actuality, hence one inseparable from the Nothing itself. This is a Nothing that dawns ever more decisively in this tradition, and if it is only fully thought in Schelling, Hegel, and Kierkegaard, it is decisively enacted in Nietzsche and Heidegger, an enactment inseparable from everything that here can be realized as liberation. Thus the Nothing is truly essential to an ultimate liberation, hence its centrality in our deepest mystical enactments, and just as Eckhart is truly primal for Schelling, Hegel, and Heidegger, he is most deeply so in knowing Godhead itself as the Nothing; this is an absolutely liberating nothingness, therefore an absolutely actual nothingness. Indeed, to apprehend the Nothing, even if doing so only in the deepest *Angst*, is to know a power that can shatter our deepest roots, and therefore our deepest bondage.

Now such shattering could not be a simple dissolution, could not be a simple or literal ending or death, and could not be because of the very power of an actual nothingness, a nothingness reflecting an absolute nothingness. Therefore its realization could never result in a simple dissolution, and could not do so if only because of the ultimate power of nothingness itself. While it is extraordinarily difficult to know this power, though it is purely known by Schelling and Hegel, this is a power that is inevitably apprehended in knowing or realizing *Angst*, and *Angst* is universal in a fallen world, or in a world that is the consequence of an original fall. If *Angst* is a consequence of an encounter with the Nothing, it is certainly a profound witness to an original fall, for the very power of *Angst* is inseparable from an ultimate or absolute guilt, a guilt that could only be the consequence of an original fall, and a guilt which we know as our own in deeply knowing *Angst*. Hence those thinkers who have most deeply understood *Angst*, Kierkegaard and Heidegger, have called forth the deepest understanding of responsibility itself, and have done so in their very understanding of guilt. This is not only a genuine renewal of Augustine and Paul, but even thereby a renewal of a uniquely Christian grace, the uniquely Christian grace of forgiveness, a forgiveness only actualized through the depths of guilt, and one wherein we can deeply know that which is most genuinely our own.

Significantly, it is in our great tragedies, above all in our great modern tragedies, that guilt is most overwhelming, and most overwhelming as an interior guilt calling forth the depths of the individual, an individual who is most uniquely individual in those very depths, depths which unveil an individual more decisively than anything else, so that it is not until the realization of this ultimate guilt that a uniquely individual consciousness first dawns. Augustine's *Confessions* commences this dawning, but it is Shakespearean tragedy which first profoundly embodies the truly unique individual, and does so through a tragic

action revolving around an ultimate guilt which is an ultimate responsibility, and a responsibility which can only enact itself as a tragic responsibility. But that is a tragedy releasing an ultimate assuagement
that is only possible through tragic destruction, a destruction that is
perhaps the purest witness to the Nothing, and yet a witness unveiling
the overwhelming power of transfiguration, a transfiguration only possible through the Nothing.

Nothing has so resisted understanding as has tragedy itself, perhaps
because we so resist understanding the Nothing, but an evocation of
the Nothing does call forth a way into both Greek and modern tragedy,
and if criticism has already established *Oedipus at Colonus* as a celebration of the Nothing, we surely could understand *King Lear* as such a
celebration, and thereby become open to tragedy as an ultimate reconciliation which is an ultimate transfiguration. Certainly tragedy calls
forth the ultimate power of an absolute negativity, and if that negativity
ultimately derives from the Nothing, or from an actual realization of
the Nothing, then the positive power of the Nothing thereby becomes
manifest, and manifest in that ultimate assuagement which is unique
to tragedy. Can we understand tragic assuagement as an enactment of
an absolute forgiveness, or of an apocalyptic forgiveness, a forgiveness
that is an apocalyptic *coincidentia oppositorum*, a coincidence of absolute destruction and absolute fulfillment, wherein each is wholly unreal
apart from the other? If we can understand that tragedy evolved out of
primordial sacrifice, and that tragic action is at bottom a sacrificial action, and an action realizing a total presence, is that the total presence
of an absolute transfiguration only made possible by the Nothing itself?

Tragedy is the deepest and purest enactment of *Angst* that we have
been given, and tragedy is not deeply understood until the advent of
German Idealism, for Aristotle's understanding of tragedy fails to rise
above the level of the tragic chorus, and tragedy must finally be alien
to a world that cannot know *Angst*. The soliloquies of *Hamlet* are quite
possibly our purest embodiment of *Angst*, an embodiment inseparable
from the deepest enactment of an individual and interior consciousness, an *Angst* inevitably breaking that consciousness in what is a truly
tragic self-negation, one making possible the depths of tragic assuagement or transfiguration. But that assuagement is inseparable from an
enactment of the depths of *Angst*, or an embodiment of the depths of
nothingness itself, depths released in the fullness of *Angst* unknown and
unmanifest apart from that release. Thus it is in our greatest tragedy

that we can encounter an ultimate transfiguration only made possible by an embodiment of *Angst*, and even if this is a veiled or masked embodiment, as it is in Greek tragedy, tragedy is nonetheless such an embodiment, and only thereby can it effect an ultimate reconciliation or atonement.

Atonement has become our most difficult and even impenetrable theological category, but it is clear that it is inseparable from an original or an absolute forgiveness, a forgiveness inseparable from an absolute destruction or absolute death. Death itself is nowhere more purely realized than it is in *Angst*, so that *Angst* cannot be dissociated from an ultimate or actual realization of death. Here, Heidegger has given us our deepest understanding, but this is finally an understanding of atonement itself, an atonement effected through a total realization of death, a death calling forth an ultimate *Angst* that is surely impossible apart from such a realization. Could it be that an original atonement is the ultimate source of *Angst*, an atonement that is absolute forgiveness: absolute forgiveness of the depths of evil, which are depths of nothingness itself, and depths inevitably calling forth *Angst* itself, an *Angst* which is an ultimate summons to an ultimate reconciliation, or to an absolute transfiguration? Is this why we so profoundly resist a deeper understanding of *Angst*, an understanding that would decisively actualize such a summons, and therefore challenge us far more profoundly than anything else, a challenge inevitably posing an ultimate Either/Or?

—September 2006

10

POSTMODERNITY AND GUILT

Is guilt nameable in a postmodern world, or even speakable as a guilt
that is an actual guilt, and actual as an interior and individual guilt?
Is the very advent of postmodernity the advent of a world or horizon in
which the interior itself becomes exterior, or undergoes a metamorphosis by passing into a truly new totality, a totality wherein there is no distinction whatsoever between interior and exterior? Thereby what was
once actual as interiority would not only become truly anonymous, but
ultimately groundless as interiority itself, a groundlessness foreclosing
any possible realization other than an exterior realization. Every such
exterior realization must inevitably foreclose the possibility of any internal or interior ground, and thus foreclose the possibility of an interior and individual guilt, but this foreclosure need not mean an actual
dissolution of guilt, for it could well make possible a transfiguration of
guilt, a transfiguration wherein an interior guilt is truly exteriorized,
thus embodied in a truly new totality.

That guilt which we once knew so deeply, a truly interior and individual guilt, is inseparable from an interior and individual impotence
in the very depths of the will itself, thereby calling forth the actuality
of an individual will that is free and impotent at once, and if this is
the only freedom of the will that we have actually known and realized,
it is a freedom truly conjoined with an interior impotence or guilt, so
that here the fullest expressions of freedom are wholly conjoined with
the fullest realizations of guilt, as fully manifest in a uniquely modern
tragic hero or heroine. Now such tragedy is impossible if only because

an individual freedom is impossible, or an individual freedom is impossible which is an interiorly enacted or realized freedom, an interior domain that is now being fully exteriorized, thereby ending every possible interior actuality that is interior and interior alone. But that is not a simple ending but far rather a transfiguration, and not only a transformation of the interior into the exterior but an ultimate transformation of every interiority we have known, so that this very interiority now becomes the opposite of itself, giving birth to an absolutely new guilt, even if a wholly nameless guilt.

Now guilt is universal as it never was before, for if once we knew that all humanity is a guilty and fallen humanity, now we know a totality that is far beyond humanity as a truly negative totality, a beyondness foreclosing the possibility of knowing this totality as a fallen or guilty totality, so that now the very language of guilt and evil is foreclosed by the disappearance of its deepest ground. Nevertheless a truly new impotence is now manifest, and one far more universal than any impotence we knew before, and if guilt itself is now disappearing, this very disappearance is releasing a total impotence that is absolutely new, and absolutely new as an all-comprehending impotence.

So it is that an ancient melancholy is passing into a truly new depression, a depression wholly beyond all possible individual enactment, and hence beyond all individual responsibility, but precisely thereby it is all comprehensive as melancholy cannot be, a comprehensiveness reflecting that new totality embodying an absolute transfiguration of all interior domains, as now an interior negativity truly and actually becomes all in all. Historically, this is absolutely new, so that we can truly know that an end of the world is now occurring, and the end of that world that once was our own, even our own in our individual guilt and impotence, an impotence and guilt that is no more, and is no more because now it is absolutely universal. Perhaps nowhere is this universality more openly manifest than in the transformation of our language and consciousness of guilt, and if guilt is now actually unspeakable, or unspeakable as an interior and individual guilt, thereby is born a truly new innocence, but an innocence wholly conjoined with a universal and total impotence.

Guilt was once an expression of an ultimate and comprehensive self-laceration, a self-laceration that is an internal and individual self-negation, yet what we once knew as an individual and interior freedom is truly and fully conjoined with such self-negation because it is inseparable from a continual enactment of itself, and hence a continual negation of that which is other than itself. Here, that which is most other than itself is most deeply within; it is not an exterior ground that is negated in the realization of interior freedom, it is far rather an interior ground, that very interior ground that is wholly other than oneself. Hence an interior and individual freedom is only possible as a consequence of an ultimate self-division, a dichotomy of consciousness that we have known as self-consciousness, and a self-consciousness only possible when consciousness can realize its own other, an other that is truly the otherness of oneself. Self-consciousness itself is inseparable from the realization of that otherness, or impossible apart from a doubling of consciousness itself; that is a doubling making possible all interior conflict, which is most deeply a conflict with oneself, and only that conflict makes possible what we have known as an individual and interior freedom.

Hence that freedom cannot be dissociated from guilt, and from an individual and interior guilt, so that the absence of that guilt is a decisive sign of the absence of such freedom, an absence inseparable from a truly new impotence. One of the many ironies of our situation is the very ubiquity of our language about freedom, yet clearly this is not an actual language but only a comprehensive chatter, a chatter divorced from every genuine consciousness of freedom, as manifest not only in our politics and mass media but in our religious life as well, or in all that religious life that is publicly manifest. Perhaps nothing is more revealing of this religious life than the absence of all sense of damnation, a damnation once known to be universal as a consequence of the fall, and a damnation which is the source of an absolute guilt. Not only is an absolute guilt now totally absent, but so too is an actual guilt, an absence which can be known as marking the disappearance of all we once knew as freedom itself.

The first actual language of interior freedom was given us by Paul, who thereby gave us our first actual language of interior and individual guilt, eventually making possible the Augustinian theological revolution, which established a uniquely Western language and understanding of self-consciousness. This in turn made possible a uniquely modern literature and art as well as a uniquely modern philosophy; each revolved about a uniquely modern center or subject, and each realized a totality of that subject or center, a totality that is now truly reversing itself. Nowhere is this reversal more openly manifest than in the advent of a consciousness that is free of all actual guilt. This is not to be confused with a consciousness that is simply innocent of guilt or one that has never been open to guilt, for this is a new postmodern condition, one only possible as a consequence of the ending of modernity, and hence the ending of a uniquely modern or post-classical guilt, an ending making possible a truly new innocence.

Yet this new innocence is inseparable from a new impotence, an impotence never known before, and one simply impossible for a consciousness that has never been a totally guilty consciousness, one whose reversal issues in this new innocence. So it is that this new innocence is a new shallowness, one in which depth itself has passed into a new and all comprehensive surface, a surface wholly without depth and precisely thereby a truly anonymous surface, a surface which is absolutely anonymous, thereby ushering in a truly new world. Now power and impotence are indistinguishable, or rather not only is power now absolutely other than freedom, but absolutely other than any possible interiority, it is a purely exterior power, and it is only as such that power can now be actual and real. Nowhere is this more fully manifest than in our public domains, in which there is only the simulacrum of freedom, and only the simulacrum of individuality and interiority as well, and if these are truly innocent domains, they are innocent only as the consequence of the absence of freedom, an absence of freedom which is the absence of guilt.

Guilt was once the consequence of the acceptance or willing of an ultimate responsibility, an individual responsibility that can never be fulfilled, hence it inevitably gives birth to a truly individual guilt, a guilt that is mine and mine alone, following a responsibility that is mine and mine alone. This responsibility can know a responsibility for every actual act, hence it can know a responsibility for every evil act that has occurred; this issues in a totally guilty consciousness, and totally guilty because it is a totally responsible consciousness. The masters of our interior domains are the deepest witnesses to such a totally responsible consciousness or conscience, and these include figures not only as opposite as Paul and Nietzsche, but as extraordinarily divergent as Shakespeare and Dostoevsky, or Kierkegaard and Proust, and if their work has given us our most profound portrait of guilt, that is a portrait inseparable from an absolute responsibility that is an absolute freedom.

Now it is an absolute responsibility that most deeply knows guilt. Here guilt is a consequence of life itself, or of a life that is a truly responsible life, a life accepting full responsibility for its every act, and for all the consequences of each act. That responsibility is freedom itself, a freedom that is an interior and individual freedom, and one that cannot be dissociated from an interior and individual guilt that is an inevitable consequence of a full responsibility for one's every act. This responsibility, in its depths, knows a full responsibility for every act that has ever occurred, as most purely enacted in Nietzsche's vision of Eternal Recurrence, and just as Nietzsche is our greatest modern master of guilt, along with Kierkegaard, a simple reversal of either Kierkegaard or Nietzsche can issue in that new innocence that now abounds among us. Is this in fact what has occurred? Was it a reversal of the very depths of late modernity that made possible the advent of postmodernity?

One decisive sign of late modernity is a wholly new consciousness of evil, an evil now known as an absolute evil precisely because it is known as an absolute nothingness. Thereby disappears all understanding of evil as a privation of the good, and now and for the first time an absolute evil can be known as inseparable from Godhead itself. Now it is impossible to think of God, or to think deeply or purely of God, without thinking of evil, and only now is a genuine or comprehensive theodicy born, one occurring not only in German Idealism but in a truly new poetry and imaginative vision, wherein an ultimate evil can be known and celebrated as an inevitable consequence of life and energy itself. So, too, does guilt realize a truly new identity in late modernity, and not only in its new and comprehensive depths, but in a truly new reconciliation or transfiguration made possible only in those depths, as profoundly enacted by Blake, Goethe, and Hegel, and if this issues in the ecstatic celebration of a Nietzsche or a Mallarmé, this is nonetheless the ending of an old world, an ending only universalized in our own time in the very advent of postmodernity.

Certainly postmodernity is not a return to a primordial innocence or to an initial or original humanity; indeed, it is not a return at all but a forward movement into a truly new world. Thus it is not only the consequence of the ending of modernity, but it is a metamorphosis of late modernity itself, and a metamorphosis of the most purely negative forces in late modernity. As these forces burn themselves out, they call forth their own integral opposites, opposites now realized not only as a new innocence, but as a new and truly universal shallowness or surface, and a surface in which depth itself is simply impossible. In no way is this to be confused with an archaic or primitive condition; it is rather the very opposite of that condition, and opposite not only in the ubiquity of a language of signs as opposed to a language of symbols, but in a truly new society and communication, one wholly artificial from every previous point of view, virtually empty of everything once manifest as humanity itself.

But is this new humanity truly innocent? Above all is it innocent of evil, or innocent of a willed or enacted evil, an evil for which one could be genuinely responsible? No one believes that evil has now come to an end, but does evil exist in that which is truly or genuinely postmodern, or that which is actually our new world and our seemingly truly new consciousness? Is not evil far rather a vestige of the past, a past that is no longer actual but nonetheless lingers in memories and echoes that bind only those who are not yet fully postmodern? We can observe the fascinating paradox that the most religious nation in the modern Western world, the United States of America, is the fullest embodiment of postmodernity, and yet here religion is more "traditional" than anywhere else in the West. Has this very conjunction of religion with a genuine postmodernity issued in a "traditional" religion freed of all actual religious or sacred tradition, and most manifestly so in its freedom from an ultimate guilt, or from any actual guilt or actual responsibility at all? Certainly this new religion is a new mass religion, and hence one liberated or divorced from everything that we have known as an individual and interior freedom, or a truly individual conscience.

Consequently, our new and seemingly powerful contemporary expressions of religion are not only innocent of guilt but innocent of freedom as well, for never since the ending of the medieval world has a religious world been so closed to freedom, and not only closed to the freedom of thinking and of speech, but closed to that freedom which is a reflection of a full responsibility, or a freedom that is responsibility itself. Indeed, nowhere in our world is there a more open or manifest abnegation of responsibility than in our religious world or worlds, nowhere else is genuine knowledge more openly slighted or ignored, and nowhere else can we encounter such a comprehensive proliferation of premodern language and understanding. Here lies our deepest opposition not only to modern science but to any genuine form of modern thinking, so that not only has theology itself virtually come to an end in these worlds, but so too has ended everything that is recognizable as art, and anything elsewhere manifest as freedom. Do not our new religious worlds approximate the world of Dostoevsky's Grand Inquisitor, and do they not offer a peace or redemption that is possible only through the loss of freedom, or the loss of every freedom that is not the freedom of obedience?

While postmodernity is seemingly making it impossible to speak of God, or to speak of God through a real and actual language, here too a metamorphosis of late modernity is at hand, a late modernity that in its depths could know the God that has been given us as abstract Spirit or the Bad Infinite, or an absolute No-saying alone, or as that Moby Dick who is a wholly alien absolute nothingness. This is the God whose death is first enacted by Blake, an enactment realizing the now vacuous body of God as Satan, a Satan whose full epiphany only occurs in late modernity, an epiphany so comprehensive as to realize absolute nothingness itself as a wholly embodied totality. If *Finnegans Wake* is an epic enactment of this totality, therein we can see and hear the actual ending of our former world and the actual dawning of a truly new world. Is God nameable in that world, nameable through any divine name or image that we have been given, or must God now inevitably be a truly or purely anonymous God?

Here the relationship between late modernity and postmodernity is decisively important, for if it is a metamorphosis of the late modern epiphany of God which is realized in the advent of postmodernity, and a metamorphosis of the depths of that Godhead, this could only be a metamorphosis of the totally alien God, of that absolute Other which is most profoundly the absolute otherness of itself; yet it is the transfiguration of this otherness alone that ultimately makes possible the birth of this new world. Such a transfiguration can concretely be apprehended in the most influential theology of the twentieth century, the theology of the early Barth, one proposing an absolute antithesis between the God of religion and the God of faith, or the God of law and the God of grace, an antithesis demanding an absolute shattering or dissolution of the God of religion, even if that God comprehends every God who has been historically known as God. The God of religion is clearly the late modern God, but this is the God who most clearly and most decisively can now be known, whereas the God of grace is the truly hidden God, known in a faith that is faith and faith alone.

It would be tempting to think that the Barth of the *Church Dogmatics* is our deepest postmodern theologian, but his is the most traditional of all of our real theologies and the one most removed from the actualities of our world. The truth is that we are bereft of a genuine postmodern theology, and perhaps bereft of a genuine postmodern literature and philosophy as well. What we far rather confront is a truly new void, a truly new vacuity or emptiness, but an emptiness now becoming a genuine totality and doing so in our very midst. Is a theological response possible to that totality, and could it include an actual language of guilt, and one in genuine continuity with all that we have known and realized as guilt? Late modernity has been a primary if not the primary site of ultimate guilt, only here is such guilt called forth philosophically, as in Nietzsche and Heidegger, and only then does it pass into the purest language, as in Kafka and Beckett. So if it is a metamorphosis or transfiguration of this guilt that has occurred in the advent of postmodernity, could the innocence of postmodernity be an absolutely alien or an absolutely impotent innocence, and one inseparable from the metamorphosis of absolute otherness?

Not even ancient Gnosticism could know such ultimate depths of an absolutely alien God as are called forth in late modernity, an epiphany inducing many servants of faith into a new silence about God, and one that has not yet abated, as fully manifest in contemporary theology and biblical scholarship. But is such silence actually possible, and above all actually possible in the new world of postmodernity? It would far rather appear that here silence is actually impossible, and more impossible now than ever previously, or is the very noise of postmodernity a truly new silence? And is this a new silence not only disguising a new impotence, but a new guilt as well, a guilt that can only express itself in a cacophonous noise, one truly cryptic to all but nonetheless truly meaningful to its enactors, who thereby are genuinely assuaged? Could a new kind of atonement be occurring in such language, one that is truly a metamorphosis of a uniquely late modern atonement, an atonement that is finally the atonement of Godhead itself?

If only because late modernity has been so little investigated theologically, it is extraordinarily difficult to respond to this question, but it is clear that such an atonement occurs in the deeper vision of Blake and the deeper thinking of Hegel, and perhaps even occurs throughout late modernity, which could well account for the truly and ultimately negative epiphanies of God that occur in that world. The truth would appear to be that guilt is deepest and purest in the very enactment of atonement, as this is fully clear in the most powerful language of Paul, who created a Christian theology of atonement. Heidegger has given us the deepest philosophical response to Paul, or at least the deepest in the twentieth century, and all too significantly philosophical interpreters of *Being and Time* have continually failed to understand its enactment of an ultimate guilt, perhaps because atonement is commonly so alien to the philosophical mind. Yet an atonement surely occurs here, one making possible the ultimate affirmations of this work, and one that perhaps occurs again in the late Heidegger's ecstatic enactments of *Ereignis*, for these could be theologically understood as enactments of the apocalyptic atonement of the uniquely Christian God.

While Heidegger can be understood as the most deeply theological of all twentieth-century philosophers, in no other truly major philosopher does there occur such an abatement of all actual language about God, and if he only actually speaks of God in the posthumously published *Beiträge*, this could account for his refusal to publish this overwhelmingly important work in his own lifetime. All too significantly, here all language about God is a truly negative language, and if this language is directed solely to the uniquely Christian God, this openly occurs in the deep emphasis in *Beiträge* on the abandonment of Being, one that first occurred in Christianity with its absolutely transcendent God, an abandonment in which Being abandons beings, but this abandonment is the fundamental event in our history, and one that is now being reversed in the apocalyptic advent of *Ereignis*. That advent is surely an atoning advent, one that is inevitably an atonement of the absolutely transcendent God, hence the profound theological offense of the late Heidegger, which can be understood as a genuinely Pauline offense.

It is only the late Heidegger who is the truly or fully apocalyptic Heidegger, and if thereby he becomes an even more purely Pauline thinker, this is a truly new theological thinking, and one with no counterpart in the world of theology. Is it here that Heidegger most deeply thinks atonement, and does so in genuine continuity with his great predecessors, Hegel and Nietzsche, an atonement that could finally only be the atonement of Godhead itself—as first philosophically enacted by Hegel, revolutionizing the whole world of philosophy? For the enactment of the death of God in Hegel means no less than this; it is an enactment only possible when Absolute Spirit has become an absolutely dichotomous Spirit, wholly and totally alienated from itself, yet it is that absolute self-alienation that makes possible the absolute self-negation of Spirit, a self-negation that is finally the source of all life and movement. Hegel, too, is an apocalyptic philosopher, and perhaps most deeply so in his very enactment of the death of God in the *Phenomenology of Spirit*, an enactment that is the ultimate source of an absolutely new world and is at bottom an atoning enactment, enacting a self-negation that is finally a self-atoning of Absolute Spirit.

Now guilt, an absolute guilt, undergoes an ultimate or absolute metamorphosis or transfiguration, a transfiguration wherein guilt becomes the very opposite of itself and does so by passing into an absolute grace. This, too, is a deeply Pauline thinking, for a Pauline grace occurs only by way of a transfiguration of ultimate guilt, as apart from that guilt grace itself is wholly meaningless and unreal. But if an atonement of God is wholly closed to Paul, it becomes inevitable as a consequence of the realization of the death of God, a realization first philosophically occurring in Hegel. Only as a consequence of the death of God is it truly possible to know God as abstract Spirit or the Bad Infinite, for it is in that death that Godhead is most absolutely alienated from itself, and only that absolute self-alienation makes actually possible an absolute self-negation or self-emptying that is not only the center but the deepest ground of a uniquely Hegelian thinking. But that thinking is not confined to Hegel, for it ever more comprehensively passes into the fullness of modernity, where it realizes truly opposite modes, opposite modes which become the driving force of late modernity, a force finally issuing in an apocalyptic explosion.

Postmodernity is a consequence of that explosion, as now a truly new humanity and new world has been born, but a new world impossible apart from the apocalyptic explosion of modernity itself, one not only ending modernity but also realizing a postmodernity that is a metamorphosis of the most negative expressions of modernity, and expressions that here pass into their very opposite. So it is that the devastating guilt of a late modernity passes into a new innocence, but a new innocence that just because it is a metamorphosis of that guilt is a new and ultimate impotence, an impotence freezing everything that once was life, and issuing in an infinite series of simulacra of life itself. Yes, those simulacra are innocent, but this is an innocence that is a purely surface innocence, one foreclosing the possibility of depth, a foreclosure that is inseparable from this innocence itself. Is this a humanity truly liberated from guilt, and thereby liberated from all deep or ultimate illusion, which is a consequence of being liberated from depth itself? Or is it far rather the most enslaved humanity that has yet come forth, one most truly and comprehensively impotent, and one most profoundly closed to the possibility of transfiguration?

Now if Paul is the first purely apocalyptic thinker, the first thinker of an apocalyptic transfiguration, is it possible to express our contemporary situation in a Pauline language, even in a Pauline language of guilt and grace? One possible point of coincidence is that Paul could know his actual historical world as a world of apocalyptic darkness, and a world even now coming to an end. It is precisely in the deepest darkness of that world, or in its deepest sin, that an apocalyptic grace is realized, and a grace which is an absolute transfiguration of sin, or of absolute guilt itself. That grace occurs in the Crucifixion, a crucifixion that is the very center of Pauline thinking, a crucifixion in which an absolute death occurs, but a death that is an absolutely atoning death, one effecting an atonement of the ultimate depths of sin. Apart from those depths the Crucifixion is wholly unreal, just as it is unreal to Paul's Gnostic opponents, opponents who could only know a pure grace having no point of contact whatsoever with darkness or sin. As opposed to every Gnostic apprehension, a Pauline grace *is* grace only insofar as it is a transfiguration of sin and darkness, and apart from that darkness and sin it is wholly unreal. It is the deepest depths of sin that are transfigured by this grace, and only an awareness of those depths makes possible an awareness of this transfiguration, so that only the deepest guilt makes possible the deepest transfiguration, and for Paul only that transfiguration is transfiguration itself.

Could a Pauline apprehension know our contemporary innocence as an innocence masking the depths of sin? And is this innocence at bottom an ultimate guilt, perhaps the most ultimate of all guilts, and precisely because in its very innocence it is most closed to grace? Nothing more deeply aroused Paul's fury than self-righteousness, a self-righteousness so comprehensive today that it extends even beyond selfhood into the absence of all depth, an absence not only making possible a new innocence, but precluding the possibility of a centeredness that is essential to a real and actual selfhood. If that is an absence foreclosing all possibility of guilt, it precisely thereby precludes everything that Paul could know as an openness to grace, and hence could only be what Paul names as an eternal death. Yet if it is truly and actually an eternal death, then an awakening to that condition could be an awakening to the possibility of an absolute death, and an absolute death that is the Crucifixion, or is that Crucifixion which is Crucifixion and Resurrection at once.

How is it that Christianity could seemingly be so powerful in the new world of postmodernity, and powerful in its most traditional or most orthodox form? Is this wholly an illusion, or is this a decisive sign of our new world, a new world that may well be the opposite of what it appears to be? Now even if the Crucifixion is minimal or disguised in the most powerful forms of contemporary Christianity, could this be the masking of an ultimate *horror religiosus*, a masking essential to the success of Christianity today, and essential to the success of Christianity in a truly postmodern world? If this is a world wholly without an interior and individual guilt, is it by necessity thereby closed to the Crucifixion, but precisely thereby open to a total innocence or a total serenity? Is it Dostoevsky's enactment of the Grand Inquisitor, which is most prophetic of our truly contemporary world, a world in which serenity and innocence are all in all, while it is freedom itself that is now most illusory? And is it the absence of freedom that is most essential not only to the success of Christianity today, but to every possible success in our world, or every possible actual realization?

Yet it may well be that the very comprehensiveness of our new innocence could make possible an opening to the depths of an ultimate atonement, an atonement so deep that it transcends depth itself and is only open to a surface innocence that is immune to all horror, hence immune to that *horror religiosus* which is an absolute atonement. Now if it is true that the great body of Christianity has been closed to the depths of Christianity itself, our contemporary Christianity and contemporary world would be in continuity with that body, but if now there is a new freedom from all depth, that freedom can be understood as an expression of a new innocence that in its very innocence could be free of barriers to depth, and thereby if only momentarily open to depth. Could that now occur so as to make possible a new and far more comprehensive or far more universal voyage into the depths, a voyage into the depths of an absolute atonement? Thus far only a few have been able to enter that enactment as it occurs in a Blake or Hegel, or a Joyce or Heidegger, but could this now become a voyage for all, and precisely because of our new innocence?

Perhaps the decisive question here is the question of guilt, and just as the shallowness of the contemporary world has given us our shallowest image and understanding of guilt, could that be essential to a new opening to guilt, even to an absolute guilt, that absolute guilt that is the guilt of Godhead itself? Few are even aware of such guilt despite its primal importance in virtually all of the most powerful enactments of late modernity, yet this innocence could be essential to an opening to that guilt, and essential to a solitary voyage that undergoes a metamorphosis into a universal voyage into the depths. Dante's *Commedia* is a truly important witness here, for in it a solitary voyage becomes a universal voyage, and does so by creating that mimesis that is an absolutely new realism, and a new realism imaginatively enacting for the first time truly actual individuals. Indeed, it is fantasy itself which first ends in the *Commedia*, and thereafter it will be absent from all of our genuine literature, or absent as a fantasy that is not a realistic fantasy. Perhaps the very proliferation of fantasy in postmodernity is a preparation for a new and universal realistic voyage; such fantasy by its very immersion in illusion could prepare us for a true break from illusion by sickening us of illusion itself. Thereby we may even lose our illusion of innocence, a loss essential to a realistic voyage, and certainly essential to any voyage into depth.

Blake's witness, too, is essential here, a Blake who gave us our purest vision of innocence, but an innocence inevitably and necessarily becoming experience, finally becoming an experience of the absolute atonement of Godhead itself. This atonement is what Blake apocalyptically enacted as the "Self-Annihilation of God," but that is a self-annihilation now occurring in everyone, that everyone who is Here Comes Everybody. It may well be that the innocence of a new postmodernity is a protection from that self-annihilation, just as our new shallowness may well be necessary to shield us from the actuality of our condition, but these can finally only be temporary expedients, only temporary assuagements of our mortal condition. True, they may be necessary to prepare us for our ultimate voyage, but that voyage even now is occurring, and occurring as a universal voyage, a voyage affecting each and every one of us, and even if this is now only manifest in a universal shallowness, that shallowness will inevitably disintegrate, and in that cataclysm each of us will undergo a self-emptying or self-negation, one that will hopefully be atoning, thus enacting an absolute and universal atonement.

—FEBRUARY 2005

11

THE EPIC VOYAGE INTO APOCALYPSE

As we descend into that darkness which is now engulfing us, do we therein encounter that ground which is our ultimate source, a ground disappearing into silence and invisibility with the full realization of our destiny? Epic voyages into darkness as enacted in the Christian epic tradition, a tradition initiated by Dante and consummated in Joyce, are voyages at once realizing a cosmic and an interior destiny, a destiny that becomes ever more comprehensive and universal as it evolves. Yet truly epic descents into darkness are simultaneously or inevitably ascents into light, a light whose splendor and glory is a full reversal of the depths and abyss of darkness. Therefore a Christian epic movement into darkness is finally and necessarily a movement into light, as the depths of darkness are here a darkness fully visible, and a darkness truly opening the actual possibility of an apocalyptic day. The glorious light of that day realizes a resurrection which is not only the culmination of a descent into Hell, but a fulfillment of a cosmic and interior abyss and chaos, one only realized through this voyage. Hence the Christian epic voyage is a fully dialectical one, a voyage in which the realization of darkness is finally the realization of light, and in which the realization of chaos and abyss is inseparable from the realization of an ultimate and final glory. Just as the *Paradiso* is wholly unreal apart from the *Inferno*, paradise regained is impossible apart from paradise lost, and Jerusalem remains truly inactual apart from Satan and Hell, even as the resurrection of Anna Livia Plurabelle is ultimately indistinguishable from the crucifixion of Here Comes Everybody.

121

That which most clearly and decisively distinguishes the Christian epic from every other epic is that its voyage occurs in an interior world that is a historically actual world, a world born in the absolutely new mimesis of Dante's *Inferno*, and culminating in the absolutely prosaic mimesis of Joyce's *Finnegans Wake*. Now if it is impossible to read *Ulysses* and *Finnegans Wake* apart from the *Commedia*, it is impossible to read Blake's epics apart from *Paradise Lost*, for each Christian epic is a renewal of its predecessor, and a renewal recreating its predecessors in a truly new world. Here, that new world is finally an apocalyptic world or totality, for the Christian epic is a deeply apocalyptic epic, continually enacting a total voyage from genesis to apocalypse, a voyage reenacting every fundamental moment and movement in that voyage. As Kierkegaard knew so deeply, a Christian repetition profoundly differs from a pagan recollection in being a forward rather than a backward movement to eternity, and a forward movement by way of an actual mimesis, a mimesis profoundly and universally occurring in the Christian epic, and occurring so as to finally realize apocalypse. This is a uniquely Christian apocalypse in its full historical actuality, so that the voyage of the *Commedia* is earthly and heavenly at once, even as it is historical and apocalyptic simultaneously, and it is realized with an exact precision and an organic comprehensiveness going far beyond anything present in its classical and biblical sources.

Consequently, possibility and actuality here fundamentally coincide, for the Christian epic realizes a pure actuality or *actus purus* which is at once the fullness of the depths of self-consciousness and the fullness of a genuinely historical destiny and world. Moreover, the *Commedia* realizes a *coincidentia* between the depths of God and the actualities of history and self-consciousness, a *coincidentia* releasing an apocalyptic Age of the Spirit, and a *coincidentia* that will explode with the birth of modernity, as enacted in *Paradise Lost*. While the *Commedia* is the summa of the Christian Middle Ages, it is even thereby a dynamic and revolutionary totality, a totality which in realizing the fullness of its own world releases an energy and power without boundaries or limits. This is because of its ground in the infinite depths of God, depths that are here actually envisioned for the first time in history, and envisioned in our first total epic, or first actual vision of totality itself. The cosmic and organic order of the *Commedia* is renewed and reborn in *Paradise Lost*, but reborn in a uniquely modern infinity, an infinity that is the infinity of the world or the universe itself, hence an infinity accompanied by an absolutely new vision of Satan and Hell. Only now do Satan and Hell threaten to become all in all, issuing in Blake's epic enactment of the totality of Satan and Hell, wherein Dante's *Commedia* is truly and actually reversed, but in a reversal renewing the *Commedia* itself.

Now it is just a historical realization of totality that embodies apocalypse, one occurring in the advent of Christianity, an advent issuing from the dawning of the Kingdom of God, and not a kingdom that is the monarchic reign or rule of God, but far rather an apocalyptic kingdom that is the total presence of God. This is the presence that the Christian epic renews, a renewal paralleling the total presence of God in a deeper Christian mysticism, but in its epic realization that total presence is apocalypse itself, and an apocalypse renewing a long lost original Christianity. Hence the Christian epic is inevitably a challenge to all established Christianity, and the very evolution of this epic is the evolution of a profound Christian heterodoxy, until in Blake and Joyce this heterodoxy is total, one wholly inverting and reversing all established or manifest Christianity. Yet Blake is our most Christocentric poet and visionary, and just as Blake rediscovers the apocalyptic Jesus, he rediscovers apocalypse, thereby not only renewing Dante but renewing original Christianity itself. This renewal is inseparable from the realization of a radical heterodoxy, the purest heterodoxy in Christian history, one that is even an apocalyptic heterodoxy, reversing the advent of Christian orthodoxy, which in turn had reversed an original Christian apocalypse.

Indeed, the advent of orthodoxies in Judaism, Christianity, and Islam alike are reversals of apocalypticism; in them an apocalyptic advent is transformed into an absolute transcendence, thus releasing ultimate historical transformations of Judaism, Christianity, and Islam, wholly distancing each from an original apocalypticism. While that apocalypticism was originally born in Israel, an apocalypticism out of which Christianity arose, its reversal created rabbinic or orthodox Judaism, just as the reversal of an originally apocalyptic Christianity created orthodox Christianity, and the reversal of an originally apocalyptic Islam created orthodox Islam. Nothing like this orthodoxy is found elsewhere in the history of religions, just as the God of this orthodoxy is unique in its absolute sovereignty and absolute transcendence, and all too ironically the Nietzsche of *The Anti-Christ* can know this God as the deification of nothingness, the will to nothingness pronounced holy, and it is the death or eclipse of this God that releases an ultimate or absolute nihilism. This is the death of God enacted in the modern Christian epic, one occurring in both Blake and Joyce, and this very occurrence realizes an epiphany of God as Satan, which is nothing less than the birth of the absolutely alien God, an absolutely alien God who is the consequence of the uniquely modern realization of the death of God. Already Hegel knew this profoundly, for the first philosophical realization of the death of God in the *Phenomenology of Spirit* is simultaneously the realization of totally abstract Spirit or what the *Science of Logic* can know as the Bad Infinite. At this crucial point Blake and Hegel are fully correlated with each other, although Blake can name totally abstract Spirit as Satan, a Satan who is not fully realized until the "Self-Annihilation" of God.

Nothing is more important in the Christian epic than its enactment of a Satan who is absolute evil but nonetheless a dialectical evil, one embodying an absolute fall that is finally a fortunate fall, for it initiates the actual realization of apocalypse. That apocalypse is the transfiguration of evil, or of absolute nothingness, one already envisioned in the book of Revelation, which itself is a primary source of the Christian epic. While an absolute evil is finally inexplicable in Christian theology, it is fully and comprehensively envisioned in the Christian epic, and envisioned here more fully than anywhere else in the world, which itself is a decisive sign of the deeply historical ground of the uniquely Christian epic. Now just as the *Inferno* is far more realistic than the *Purgatorio* or the *Paradiso*, the enactment of Satan in *Paradise Lost* is more realistic and more actual than its enactment of the Son of God, and Blake's epics enact evil more realistically than they enact goodness or grace. Yet it is *Ulysses* and *Finnegans Wake* that are here most challenging, for these are the most realistic of all epics, yet their enactments are seemingly beyond good and evil, for all such moral judgment now becomes impossible, as it is seemingly no longer possible actually to know either good or evil. Is this a decisive sign that these all too modern epics enact a truly nihilistic world, or is this rather a sign of a world beyond good and evil in a Nietzschean sense, one truly transcending everything that we have known as good and evil?

In a fundamental sense, such a transcendence is already present in *Paradise Lost*, as the language and imagery of this epic is the most violent and explosive language in our epic poetry, or the most explosive language that can sustain a unitary and organic mode and form. Lying at the center of *Paradise Lost* is a violent and total polarity, a polarity here realized by the polar opposition between Satan and the Son of God, and it is precisely this total opposition that gives birth to truly new epiphanies of both Satan and Messiah. For the first time in Christian poetic language, Satan is a glorious and exalted actor and speaker, and only now in Christian poetic language does the Son of God make a real and atoning movement into actual death. Thereby Satan and the Son undergo a full reversal of their manifest or traditional identities, a reversal wherein Satan becomes the dominant axial presence in this epic. Now Satan's voice is the center of a new and solitary self-consciousness, and this epiphany embodies a reversal of celestial transcendence, a reversal making possible the full and actual death of the Son. God the Father, too, undergoes a new and radical epiphany in *Paradise Lost*, an epiphany bringing to an end the presence and actuality of the Trinity in the Christian imagination. In the *Paradiso*, as in Augustine and Aquinas, it is the Trinity that is the Creator. But in *Paradise Lost* a new epiphany of the absolute sovereignty and transcendence of God makes necessary, even absolutely necessary, a retirement of the Creator in the act of creation (7:163–73).

The power and authority of absolute sovereignty cannot truly or actually be present in a wholly dichotomous world, in a world torn asunder by new and violent polarities, so that only the Son of God can now actually effect the creation, a Son who is realized in this epic as being in an integral and polar relationship with Satan, and it is only thereby that he can undergo an ultimate humiliation and death. *Paradise Lost* is not only a celebration but an actual embodiment of paradise lost, for never again in our history will a unitary cosmos actually be present in consciousness, and ever thereafter self-consciousness will deepen its dichotomous self-alienation, until it finally comes to an end. But the self-alienation of self-consciousness is finally inseparable from the end or dissolution of the Trinity in the Christian imagination, an ending which is a necessary ground for the full birth of modernity. That birth occurs only with the advent of a full and total dichotomy, a dichotomy that only now is historically actual and real, and real in both a truly new history and a truly new self-consciousness. Now an apocalyptic ending occurs of the God who is the ground of the Great Chain of Being, and an absolutely new infinite universe is actualized in consciousness, a universe wholly transcending any imaginative form or order and wholly other than the interiority of self-consciousness.

In the Enlightenment, God as God becomes manifest and real in consciousness as an empty and vacuous Supreme Being, that very God fully released by the French Revolution, whom Blake named as Satan. This is the God whom Melville epically named and enacted as Moby Dick, and it is the advent of the wholly self-alienated God which is an essential ground of the triumph of full modernity, an advent unveiling a pure dichotomy at the very center of Godhead itself, as so fully realized both by Hegel and by Blake. Indeed, it is the advent of the purely dichotomous God in history and consciousness which ushers in a truly new and uniquely modern apocalypticism, an apocalypticism fully enacted in Blake's supreme epics, and above all so in *Jerusalem*. This is an ultimately new apocalypticism that is fully realized philosophically by Schelling, Hegel, and Nietzsche, as the Age of the Spirit is fully and actually at hand, but only by way of an ultimate and eschatological realization of the death of God. Now the original apocalypticism of Christianity is recovered and renewed after it had seemingly come to an end, and even if precursors of such a renewal had occurred in innumerable radical Christian movements earlier, now a renewal of this order occurs in the fullness of history itself. Although such a fullness of history is a fullness of violence and terror, as this Age of the Spirit is simultaneously the Age of Satan, that is yet another sign of a genuinely apocalyptic age, but now one promising the apocalypse of Godhead itself.

The most radical and comprehensive expressions of mysticism can be understood as an apocalypse of the Godhead, one wherein the Godhead is wholly realized here and now, and realized in the depths of a fully actual interiority. But a mystical realization is not an apocalyptic realization, not one occurring in the actuality of history, in once and for all events that are fully historical events. A full philosophy of history is not born until German Romanticism, just as a truly historical consciousness does not occur before this, for a full historical consciousness is absent from the ancient and medieval worlds and only begins to dawn in the *Inferno*. All too significantly this dawning is simultaneously an apocalyptic dawning, thus demonstrating the integral relationship between history and apocalypse in this apocalyptic tradition, a tradition fully realized in the Christian epic, whose final expression in Joyce comprehensively realizes history as apocalypse. Throughout the movement of the Christian epic, history is ever more fully realized as apocalypse, until, with its culmination in *Finnegans Wake*, history is totally actual and totally apocalyptic at once. If this is a history that is a truly chaotic history, it is nonetheless a purely actual history, the most actual history that has ever been called forth. Joyce could know himself as a double of Blake, and we can know *Ulysses* and the *Wake* as genuine descendents or renewals of *Milton* and *Jerusalem*, and if the *Wake* and *Ulysses* together comprise a double epic, this is our fullest historical epic while simultaneously being a totally actual apocalypse.

Yet all four of these epics enact the death of God, an apocalyptic death of God realizing absolute apocalypse, or that total apocalypse which is all in all. It is just for this reason that this apocalyptic death can be known as the apocalypse of God, as Godhead itself becomes all in all through absolute apocalypse, for the "Self-Annihilation of God" is itself the apocalypse of God. This, too, is a historical apocalypse wherein the God who is God and only God comes to an end both in self-consciousness and in historical actuality, and out of this ending there issues an absolutely new totality. Thus the death of God in the modern world is an apocalyptic explosion of history and consciousness releasing the depths of the Godhead in a wholly new totality, as the dynamic and cosmic totality of the *Commedia* is now reborn and renewed by way of an absolute inversion or reversal of itself. That reversal enacts and embodies a fully actual apocalypse of God, releasing and realizing that absolute subject that is a *coincidentia oppositorum* of an interior and of an exterior totality, one that Blake could name as the *coincidentia oppositorum* of Christ and Satan, and that Joyce can enact as a *coincidentia oppositorum* of Here Comes Everybody and Anna Livia Plurabelle.

Now an absolutely new consciousness and history are fully realized, a new consciousness actually knowing itself as an infinite consciousness, and infinite both macroscopically and microscopically, as every limit and boundary separating finitude and infinity is now transcended and dissolved. Under the impact of this revolutionary transformation, the Christian epic itself is transformed so as to lose every sign or mark of a finite structure and order. Blake's apocalyptic epics are decisive embodiments of a full modernity, and if their dark chaos progressively dissolves all unitary and sequential order and form, this itself is evidence of their truly modern ground, a ground which is an actually infinite ground. But that infinite ground in its very actuality is thereby an apocalyptic ground, and just as Blake's epics fulfill and carry forward the apocalyptic voyages of the *Commedia* and *Paradise Lost*, all interior and cosmic domains now truly explode, an explosion decisively recorded and embodied in *Milton* and *Jerusalem*, and then finally and comprehensively realized in *Ulysses* and *Finnegans Wake*. Whereas chaos seemingly dominates Blake's epics, Joyce's epics realize a *coincidentia oppositorum* of a wholly unitary order and a full and actual chaos, as chaos for the first time is fully realized both internally and externally, and realized with an exactitude in *Finnegans Wake* without parallel anywhere else in the world.

The Christian epic poet as opposed to every other epic poet, or every other artist, is fully embodied in his epic, he himself is its initial if not primary actor, and although *Paradise Lost* would appear to be a decisive exception to this, that epic is impossible apart from Milton's own deeply individual theological voyage, as recorded in *De doctrina Christiana*, which was written at the same time as was *Paradise Lost*. Although beginning as an orthodox theologian, Milton became ever more decisively a heterodox theologian, as most manifest in his understanding both of the Creator and of the Son of God in the *Doctrina*, a Son whose kenotic sacrifice could not be reconciled with the absolute sovereignty of the Father, and a Father who is absolute Creator only by creating not out of nothing but out of Himself. But perhaps Milton is most heterodox in his final refusal of the Church, driving him outside of all churches, a refusal which is renewed in both Blake and Joyce, and already enacted in Dante's assault upon the Papacy. It is significant that Barth could only create neo-orthodox theology by creating a purely Church theology, the first such theology in history, and one absolutely other than the theology enacted in the evolution of the Christian epic. Milton's deep heterodoxy becomes a total heterodoxy in Blake and Joyce, and this is a heterodoxy inseparable from an absolutely new consciousness and history, a history and a consciousness in which churches become wholly alien or peripheral, as so deeply enacted in Joyce's *A Portrait of the Artist as a Young Man*. Both *Ulysses* and *Finnegans Wake* are deep enactments of Joyce himself, but thereby Joyce becomes our Everyman, an Everyman enacting our final voyage, a voyage into that darkness which is finally light.

An absolute fall is enacted upon the first page of the *Wake*, the fall of that Finnegan who is God again, and God again in his eternal condemnation and fall, a self-condemnation and self-fall, which is the deepest energy of the "humptyhillhead" or Godhead. Dante, in creating the Christian epic, created an epic vernacular language, and

Joyce ends the Christian epic by creating an epic language that is a fully and actually spoken language, a language whose actuality is inseparable from the actuality of speech itself. That actuality is a pure actuality, an *actus purus*, and an *actus purus* which is the speech of God. Therewith and thereby speech gains an actuality that is truly new, as the purely transcendent voice of God passes into the purely immanent voices of *Finnegans Wake*, voices that are the voice of everyone and everybody even while being the voice of Here Comes Everybody, or here comes God again or Finnegan. But God again is God *again*, and God again in the linguistic chaos of the *Wake*, a chaos in which the apocalypse of God is the fall of God, and the fall of God into a fully and actually spoken speech. This speech is truly eternal recurrence, the eternal recurrence of condemnation and fall, and the enactment of that fall in the pure actuality of speech. Yet that is precisely the reason why this is the apocalypse of God, and the final apocalypse of God, an apocalypse in which the fall of God in finally occurring again is reversed as fall, a reversal which occurs and is real when fall is fully and finally spoken, and thus is finally annulled.

Consequently, it is the unspeakable that ends in *Finnegans Wake*, an unspeakable that is the domain of eternal silence, and hence the domain of that Godhead which has not fully and finally spoken, or that Godhead only present in total silence. That ending can occur only by way of the apocalyptic death of God, a death of God that is the ultimate apocalypse of God, one truly ending absolute fall and thereby realizing fall itself as an absolutely fortunate fall. Nothing is more continually reenacted in *Finnegans Wake* than is the fall of God, here commonly enacted as the eternal fall of Here Comes Everybody, and that eternal fall is absolutely universal, for only through that fall does the Creator become wholly identical with the creation, and only then does *actus purus* become all in all: "Rise up now and aruse! Norvena's over" (619.28). Norvena or nirvana is over when silence finally ends, when an original silence has wholly passed into speech, a passing that is the wake of God, a wake which itself is resurrection, and an apocalyptic resurrection which is the apocalypse of God. This is that apocalypse which was first enacted and proclaimed by Jesus, then renewed in the apocalyptic Paul, thence passing into a purely dichotomous consciousness and self-consciousness, whereupon it passes into the cosmic, interior, and divine totality which is envisioned in Dante's *Commedia*, only to be repeated and renewed in the modern Christian epic.

Nothing more clearly characterizes the Christian epic than does its overwhelming authority, for not even Shakespeare or Goethe can command the authority of Dante and Milton, nor can a pope or a commissar command the authority of Joyce. Fully to hear a genuinely epic voice is to come into and under its authority, therein to be initiated into an authority that is universal and all-encompassing, and even if we have not read the *Wake*, we nonetheless have read it, for it speaks the night language or the "not language" of us all. Myth and fantasy finally end in *Ulysses* and *Finnegans Wake*, for these seemingly mythical novels are the most realistic imaginative works we have been given, realistic even in transforming myth and ritual into historical actuality, a historical actuality here becoming all in all. Thus the epic journey of the *Wake* is realized through a ritual movement, one in which the *missa solemnis* becomes the *missa jubilaea*, a *missa jubilaea* that is a cosmic and universal Eucharist, and precisely thereby is the apocalypse of God. For this is a Eucharistic feast revolving about the continual enactment of the death of its Host, a death releasing an ultimate Joy, an ultimate Joy that is absolute Yes-saying, as so profoundly foreseen and enacted by Nietzsche himself. Accordingly, it is Nietzsche and not Aquinas who provides the philosophical ground of Joyce, and if Eternal Recurrence is fully and finally celebrated in the *Wake*, this is an eternal recurrence of that Easter which is Good Friday, or that crucifixion which is eternal resurrection.

Now darkness falls upon all light and night is everywhere, but that night releases an ecstatic joy, a joy that is celebrated in the final episodes of *Ulysses* and *Finnegans Wake*. This is the ecstatic joy embodied in a new Jerusalem, that very Jerusalem who is epically named and envisioned by Blake, and who had earlier been enacted as Dante's Beatrice, but who only now becomes fully embodied in Molly Bloom and Anna Livia Plurabelle. Only now does the Mother of God speak in the night language of our world, a night language perhaps originally present in a Tantric or Vajrayana Hinduism and Buddhism, a night language that is now and for the first time the language of all and everyone. Yet only now does Christianity fully realize and enact its own original ground, an enactment that brings Christian history or Christendom to an end, finally actualizing the wake or ending of the Christian Creator. That ending occurs in *Finnegans Wake*, even as it is fully anticipated in the final Yes of *Ulysses*: "Yes I said yes I will Yes." Indeed, this is the Yes of Godhead itself, an absolute Yes that is an absolute kenosis or self-emptying, which both Dante and Joyce can know as the absolutely sacrificial Mother of God. This is the mother who is both mother and daughter of the Son (*Paradiso* 33), and a mother whom Blake envisioned as the apocalyptic Christ, a mother wholly absent from *Paradise Lost*, an absence making possible an epiphany of the Father therein as absolute sovereignty and absolute sovereignty alone.

Yet that is the Father who wholly dies in the apocalypse of God, as first fully envisioned on the penultimate plate of Blake's *Jerusalem*, a death profoundly renewed in Joyce's epics, but now occurring in an apocalypse of God that is an apocalypse of all and everything. Now even as the Creator and Jerusalem are ecstatically and erotically united in the closing of *Jerusalem*, Here Comes Everybody and Anna Livia Plurabelle are so united in the closing of *Finnegans Wake*, a closing which is an opening to an absolutely new beginning, even if that beginning is a perpetual and eternally repeated wake. That wake is our wake, but is so only because it is the wake of God, a wake that is God awake or the self-emptying of God again and again and again. Or, as we hear and speak Anna Livia Plurabelle's final cry on the last page of the *Wake*:

Sad and weary I go back to you, my cold father, my cold mad father, my cold mad feary father, till the near sight of the mere size of him, the moyles and moyles of it, moananoaning, makes me seasilt saltsick and I rush, my only, into your arms. I see them rising! Sabe me from those therrble prongs! Two more. Onetwo moremens more. So. Avelaval. My leaves have drifted from me. All. But one clings still. I'll bear it on me. To remind me of. Lff! So soft this morning, ours. Yes. Carry me along, taddy, like you done through the toy fair! If I seen him bearing down on me now under whitespread wings like he'd come from Arkangels, I sink I'd die down over his feet, humbly dumbly, only to washup. Yes, Tid. There's where. First. We pass through grass behush the bush To. Whish! A gull. Gulls. Far calls. Coming, far! End here. Us Then. Finn, again! Take. Bussofthee, mememormee! Till thousendsthee. Lps. The keys to. Given! A way a lone a last a loved a long the

—MARCH 2008

12

ADIEU

The Call to Radical Theology

The apocalyptic transfiguration of Godhead has been my deepest theological commitment as a radical theologian, and I wonder how this could be a truly new theological motif, for such transfiguration is at the very center of modern apocalyptic thinking and vision, even if it is ignored by the whole world of theology. Indeed, the worlds of both philosophy and theology virtually ignore the ultimate problem of evil as an untouchable subject, and perhaps untouchable because if genuinely posed, it must inevitably ask whether radical or absolute evil is embodied in God. While this is absolutely fundamental for Hegel, his language so disguises it that few are aware of it, and if Böhme's vision initially made this possible for Hegel, only such a ground makes possible a fully dialectical theological thinking, which is yet another reason we have never been given a fully dialectical theology. Could it be that at a time when there is so little speaking of God, or at least serious speaking of God, that an ultimate blasphemy could be even more forbidden than before, and is it possible that a full and actual speaking of God today must inevitably be blasphemous, and even ultimately blasphemous?

Already we can fully observe this in Nietzsche and Joyce, and in Kafka too, but is it possible that today this is true even in our common language and speech, or is so when that speech is fully actual or fully embodied speech? In my experience, whenever one with a genu-ine sensitivity happens to hear a television sermon, he or she hears a genuine blasphemy, even if it goes unnamed as such, a blasphemy leav-ing a nasty taste not easily forgotten. The clergy today probably have a lower general reputation than ever before, and even if this is commonly undeserved, "God-language" is offensive today, and most offensive to those who are most sensitive, or even at bottom most religious. Noth-ing more fully demonstrates this than our deeper or purer literature, and it is fascinating that two generations ago "Literature and Theol-ogy" was a rapidly advancing discipline, whereas now it has virtually disappeared.

We are coming to see all too clearly how the absence of any real understanding of ultimate evil within the whole world of theology is a truly and decisively crippling emptiness or void. But the same could be said of the world of philosophy, except for the philosophies of Hegel and Nietzsche, but this is just the point at which contemporary phi-losophy is most distant from Nietzsche and Hegel. True, in our time Alphonso Lingis cannot only think but also envision an absolute evil, but thereby Lingis is even more isolated and alone than is D. G. Leahy, and if Leahy and Lingis are now our most radical Catholic thinkers, they are also and perhaps even thereby our most solitary thinkers, and this despite the fact that Lingis has had a substantial impact, though almost no impact upon theology itself.

I now often ask myself why I write theology in a world that is so closed to theology, or closed to a genuine theology, and even if one ultimately writes to oneself, it is precisely then that one attempts to be most real, and most real in writing the impossible, but now virtually everyone thinks that the writing of theology has become impossible. While I do hope that I have at least written fragments of theology, per-haps they are fragments in a Kierkegaardian sense, which means that they have an enormous potential, even if one wholly beyond the power I have been given. But there is another and deeper sense in which our theological condition is truly unique, for despite the necessity for the-ology of a communal ground, such a communal ground now appears to be impossible for any genuinely theological thinking, and impossible if only because of the advent of a truly new world, a new atheological world, a world wholly divorced from everything that we have known as a theological ground, a literally godless world, and this despite that new "God-language" which appears to be everywhere. Is this not precisely the time in which we are most in need of an "atheistic" theology, a theology truly negating everything we have known as God, and only thereby becoming open to whatever theological possibilities actually exist for us? So perhaps a "godless" world can become the new communal or corporate ground of theology, one making possible a truly universal theology, or truly universal in this new world. Just as I believe that we are all given a theological vocation, is it possible that such a vocation is now more actual than ever before, or more necessary for anything that we can truly know as life? For ours is a world wholly empty of everything we once knew as ultimate hope or ultimate affirmation, except insofar as this seemingly occurs in a new virtual reality, and it is all too significant that it is only a virtual reality that we can know as a liberating reality.

If this is our situation, however, not only is a wholly new theology demanded, but one fully released from its previous enactments; now the very word "theology" is perhaps unusable, or possibly usable only by those profoundly conservative or reactionary currents which are now overwhelming us, giving us not genuinely conservative but rather reactionary theologies. This is most purely manifest in that radical Neoplatonism which is being reborn in our midst, and reborn by way of genuinely important thinkers such as Levinas and Derrida, so that this truly is a radical theological thinking, but one wholly remote from the actualities of our world. Thereby such thinking profoundly differs from our fundamentalisms, and if for the vast majority of us theology simply is fundamentalism, the conjunction of fundamentalism and a radical Neoplatonism gives us an either/or: either a purely reactionary or a purely otherworldly theology. Something parallel to this dilemma is also now present politically, so that ours is truly an ultimate crisis deeply affecting every dimension of our lives. If only in this perspective, perhaps the true importance of theology can once again become manifest, for theology is finally inescapable, and above all inescapable in times of ultimate crisis, so that all too clearly theology is inescapable for us.

But even if it is inescapable it may nevertheless be impossible, and above all impossible as a forward rather than a backward movement. While innumerable voices are insisting that there is no longer any real distinction between backward and forward, we can surely know our manifest theologies as backward-moving theologies, and precisely thereby theologies which must be reversed. Yet they cannot be reversed by a thinking taking us wholly outside of history and consciousness, as does every genuine Neoplatonism today; nor can they be reversed by a thinking refusing to think about God, or refusing to think about God in a contemporary language. No, we are impelled to think about God, and to think about God by way of our own horizon and world, and even if this will inevitably call forth a *horror religiosus*, that horror is now inescapable for us. This is just the point at which my own theological voyage could become manifest as a universal theological voyage, or universal within our "godless" world, and even if mine is finally an insignificant voyage, it could nevertheless be significant as a theological model, a model echoing far more profound and ultimate voyages, but echoing them in such a way as to make them open to all of us. This, I believe, is the real calling of the theologian, the theologian who is a voice of everyone, and now a voice of an apocalyptic Here Comes Everybody, an everybody who is no one and everyone at once, and yet an everybody who is undergoing an ultimate voyage, and even if this is now a voyage into the depths of emptiness and horror, it *is* an ultimate voyage, and therefore it finally releases an ultimate joy.

Despite Kierkegaard and Nietzsche, or perhaps in part because of them, a genuine singularity is truly disappearing today, a disappearance which could call forth a truly new universality, a universality only made possible by profoundly singular voyages, but the resolution of those voyages ends singularity as such. This is clearly true in our great Christian epics, just as it is true in Augustine's theological voyage, which inaugurated everything we paradigmatically know as theology today. Now if Augustine's theological voyage was from paganism to Christianity, or from an ancient world to a Christian world, is our theological voyage one from historical Christianity to a truly new world, and new not only from the perspective of Christendom but from the perspective of every previous horizon? It is precisely this newness, this *novitas mundi*, that demands a refusal of every old world, including every previous theological world or horizon. Hence a theological purgation is essential to this voyage, and just as this deeply occurs in each of our Christian epics, and occurs both comprehensively and cumulatively, a genuinely forward movement is thereby decisively manifest, even if it culminates in an eschatological and final ending.

That is an ending now calling us, but it is a truly cumulative ending, one that is the consummation of a vast and comprehensive movement, a movement which is itself fulfilled in such an ending, and

fulfilled precisely as an absolute ending. Now it is just an absolute ending that has never been realized theologically, or only realized as an
absolute beginning rather than an absolute ending, and if this is an
ending to which we are now being called, it is an ending that can only
be realized as a universal ending, and a universal ending enacted by
each and every one of us. This alone is the decisive difference between
an absolute ending and an absolute beginning, and if only God or the
Creator can enact an absolute beginning, everyone or everybody enacts
an absolute ending, an ending only possible by way of the dissolution
or transfiguration of the Creator. This is just the transfiguration that
the Christian epic enacts, and only that transfiguration makes possible
apocalypse, which is ultimately the apocalypse of God.

Ultimate or absolute apocalypse could only be the apocalypse of
Godhead itself, and if an understanding of such an apocalypse has
long been the goal of my theology, perhaps such an understanding can
only fully be realized corporately, and realized in that apocalyptic body
which is the apocalyptic body of Godhead. Blake and Joyce have given
us glorious visions of that body, and these are visions that each of us is
called upon to enact, an enactment that is our deepest realization and
one finally bringing us an ultimate joy. But that joy is inseparable from
a passage through a *horror religiosus*, a truly apocalyptic horror, and a
horror certainly embodied in our world. If even that embodiment is
the embodiment of God, and the embodiment of the darkness of God,
that darkness is absolutely essential to apocalypse, absolutely essential
to an apocalyptic transfiguration. One of the deeper motifs of my *Godhead and the Nothing* (2003) is the transfiguration of evil, a transfiguration that is finally the "self-saving" of Godhead itself, a self-saving
which is an absolute transfiguration, even an absolute transfiguration
of absolute horror. If our clearest vision of that horror is Moby Dick,
this is a genuine vision of a uniquely modern epiphany of God, one
going far beyond its ancient Gnostic counterparts as an actualization
of absolute evil, but an evil absolutely essential to genuine apocalyptic
transfiguration.

This is an ultimate theological truth that virtually everyone profoundly resists. Kierkegaard has taught us that it is the purest theology
which is the most ultimate offense, and apart from that offense theology is truly unreal, but is anything more offensive theologically than
an evocation of the absolute evil of God, and of the absolute necessity
of that evil, and its absolute necessity for apocalypse itself? Now it is

not insignificant that a genuinely apocalyptic theology has been virtually impossible; theology has primarily known redemption or salvation
as a consequence of an eternal return, one which is the very opposite
of an apocalyptic movement, and precisely as a backward movement of
return to eternity. Theology has been closed to a forward movement
to eternity, hence closed to both eschatology and apocalypse, and this
is true of our greatest theologies, the theologies of an Augustine, an
Aquinas, and a Barth. Only the most powerful Christian heterodoxies
have been truly apocalyptic. Yet if ours is an apocalyptic situation
and condition, then it is just an apocalyptic theology that could now
become real, and become real to each and every one of us.

Indeed, it could be that precisely because our given theology is a
non-apocalyptic theology that it is wholly unreal in our new world or
wholly bound to reactionary forces. We must never forget that in Judaism, Christianity, and Islam alike, normative theology, or that theology
that became the established theology, arose as a dissolution or transformation of apocalypticism, so that here theology is inseparable from
an anti-apocalypticism, and the deepest heterodoxies have largely been
apocalyptic heterodoxies. So likewise the deepest heterodoxies in the
medieval and the modern worlds have been apocalyptic heterodoxies,
and while apocalypticism can be truly demonic, as it is in Nazism and
a totalitarian Marxism, it has also given us our most ultimate hope, the
only hope that is an absolute hope. Only apocalypticism envisions an
absolute transfiguration, a transfiguration finally inseparable from the
transfiguration of Godhead itself, hence it is here and only here that we
discover absolute heterodoxies. This is a heterodoxy fully embodied in
a Hegel or a Nietzsche, but also in a Blake and a Joyce, and if it is just
here that we may discover the most profound offense, that is finally a
purely theological offense and an absolute blasphemy.

Is it possible not to be tempted by blasphemy in our world, or possible for anyone who is awake, or anyone with an ear for the actuality
of speech? And is it not true that our greatest blasphemers have been
our prophetic blasphemers, including not only Blake, Nietzsche, and
Joyce, but the earliest prophets of Israel; and if it is here that the greatest dichotomy between priestly and prophetic religion occurs, is such
blasphemy not essential to priestly religion itself? Is real humor possible
apart from blasphemy, and if it is our most terrible situations that give
rise to the deepest humor, just as it is tragedy that has given us our
purest jesters, can deep comedy exist apart from deep tragedy, or life

itself exist apart from death? All such questions have been evaded by our theologies, but can that continue to be true, for is it not the most blasphemous questions that are now the truest theological questions, those questions now most impelling a theological response? Yes, our most agonizing questions are what most impel a genuine theological language, and not only questions which are seemingly impossible questions, questions which truly assault their hearers with the most ultimate challenge, and if all such questions are dissolved in our common theology, is that not a dissolution of a real or actual humanity? Hence it is the common theology in every world that most invites blasphemy, for not only is blasphemy inseparable from a sacred or holy ground, but it can only genuinely be answered by a blasphemous theology, and by a truly or radically blasphemous theology.

If I have been given a blasphemous theology, it is just thereby that I can be most responsive to our new world. This, too, is a communal vocation, a vocation wherein one not only speaks for others, but is a voice for their speech, or is only actually a voice as the voice of others. Genuine theology is always a gift, and not only a gift of grace, but a gift of others, for it is real to the extent that it speaks for all, or speaks for all within its own horizon. Hence theology is never one's own, or is one's own only insofar as it is the consequence of a solitary exploration, but that solitude is real only insofar as it is actual for others, or actual for one's own world. This is dramatically manifest in a Kierkegaard or a Nietzsche, our most solitary thinkers, and yet those very thinkers who had the greatest impact upon those worlds which they discovered or unveiled. Yes, Nietzsche and Kierkegaard are theologians, our greatest fully modern theologians, and they have given our world its deepest theological inspiration, but thereby they are reborn in others, and reborn in new language worlds which are ever more fully universal, until finally this is a language not only for everyone but of everyone as well. One participates in that language world insofar as one speaks the language of Here Comes Everybody, a language that is the very opposite of everything given us as a common language, and opposite because it is the language of an apocalyptic humanity, or the language of a truly new world.

Now just as every given or manifest theological language is a language struggling against that world, and just thereby a backward-moving language, an apocalyptic theological language will necessarily reverse that backward movement, but this reversal is not a solitary reversal, it is one occurring in the very fullness of the world. Genuine theological languages are inevitably corporate languages, and they are languages which speak us, or speak our deeper ground, and to hear that language is to hear one's own ground, and even if it is in solitude that this language is most actual, the center of this solitude is a center that is everywhere. Even if all too indirectly and elusively, that everywhere is embodied in a genuine theological language, and while such language is commonly cryptic and fragmentary, it nonetheless is the vehicle of a true power, and a liberating as well as an enslaving power. The truth is that genuine theological language is simultaneously liberating and enslaving, far more so than any other language, and while in our world theological language is our most enslaving language, it is just thereby that a reversal of our dominant theological language can lead to liberation. So an enormous possibility is present here, the possibility of reversing a truly enslaving language, thereby an actual liberty is possible, and an actual liberty for us.

Let us remember that it is our most negative naming which issues in the fullest possibility of the most liberating transformations, so that Hegel's naming of the given or manifest God as the Bad Infinite or abstract Spirit is inseparable from an enactment of an absolute transfiguration of the totality of Spirit, just as Nietzsche's naming of that God as the will to nothingness pronounced holy is inseparable from the enactment of an apocalyptic Eternal Recurrence, an eternal recurrence which is the very opposite of an eternal return. The truth is that our most liberating language and vision is inevitably a theological language, and while it is equally true that our most enslaving language is a theological language too, it is this ultimate or absolute opposition which has engendered our deepest theological language, and our deepest visionary language as well. Truly or actually to do theology is to enact such language, and even if this occurs only in the most minimal ways, occur it does, so that an actual theological language is at least potentially explosive, and that explosion is both liberating and enslaving at once. Our world at bottom is perhaps the most anti-theological world in history, and understandably so given the dominance of enslaving theologies in our world, but these very theologies offer an enormous potential, and a truly liberating potential if these theologies can fully and finally be reversed. That has certainly been a fundamental goal of my theology, and of every contemporary theology to which

I can respond, and whether or not any actual success has here been achieved, the effort has surely been real.

So in closing these reflections, or in making my adieu, I do so by paying homage to theology, a theology which has been my deepest home, but also a thorn in my flesh that made peace impossible, even while being the source of an ultimate joy. As I have said again and again in my work, I deeply believe that all of us are called to a theological vocation, and that we inevitably exercise that vocation whether consciously or not. But this is just the reason why we can be so anti-theological, and above all so in confronting those actual theologies that are now at hand, as commonly these are little more than parodies of liberation or enlightenment, and when genuine expressions of power do occur, they are almost invariably cryptic or fragmentary. This power does demand an enactment on the part of the hearer, for it is only in enactment that theology is real. Hence theology, as opposed to poetry or philosophy, is only real in its enactment, an enactment which is a bodily enactment in the here and now. In this sense and in this sense only, every theology is a corporate theology, or even a church theology, but here the church is the very body of the world, or the body of that Buddha or Christ who is totally incarnate, including in the emptiness and the horror of our world.

Must theology now say an adieu to God, and not simply to that God whom we have actually known, but to any God whatsoever, or to any God who can be spoken or named? This is perhaps our most challenging theological question, and it is one that we invariably ask in confronting the crisis of theology, and theology is only real today insofar as it is in crisis. Many take comfort in a mystical dissolution of every idea and image of God, a dissolution occurring in the dark night of the soul, but one which is an essential purgation making possible a full union with the Godhead. No doubt a genuine mysticism will always be a possibility for us, and perhaps most so in the darkest of times, but the truth is that few of us have received a mystical gift, so that this is a way only for the very few. Must the rest of us now say goodbye to God, and not only say it but enact it, and enact it in the fullness of our lives? This is just what Nietzsche's madman apprehended in his proclamation of the death of God, and if that is as deep a prophecy as we have ever been given, it is finally inseparable from Nietzsche's prophetic enactment of Eternal Recurrence. Eternal recurrence is an absolute immanence, but only insofar as absolute transcendence is apocalyptically transfigured into absolute immanence. Yes, God is dead in that immanence, but that immanence is an absolute transfiguration of God, hence this death is a Hegelian negation, for it preserves what it negates, but preserves it only in a wholly transfigured form or expression.

Is that what our adieu to God must now be? Can we truly say our adieu to God only by hallowing that Name, and is it by dissolving that Name that we truly hallow it, so that now we can enact the Lord's Prayer only by dissolving the divine Name? There is an enormous body of modern prophecy and vision enacting such a dissolution, but the remarkable fact is that this dissolution does preserve the name of God, and preserves it even in our desert, so that it is a Nietzsche or a Blake who most forcefully speaks the name of God in our world, and this is an ultimate language and speech which has been given to us all. Yes, our true prophecy is always a prophecy of God, and is so even when it is a prophecy of the death of God, and when this prophecy is an apocalyptic prophecy, as it is in both Blake and Nietzsche, it is a prophecy of an absolute transfiguration. Here not only does everything flow into everything else, but everything *is* everything else, and is everything else through that death of God which is the transfiguration of God, and therein the transfiguration of everything whatsoever. This is the New Jerusalem we have been promised, but it can occur only when we have made our adieu to God, or rather only when we accept that adieu to God which Godhead itself has given us in this apocalypse.

—MARCH 2005

APPENDIXES

Appendix A

The Gospel of Christian Atheism Reexamined

The Gospel of Christian Atheism was written in 1965 and was intended to mediate an American radical theology to the public at large, although its author had no expectation of the public furor that would arise in the following year over the advent of a death of God theology. When this book was written I had not yet found a publisher for my Blake book, *The New Apocalypse: The Radical Christian Vision of William Blake* (1967), so that this became an occasion for a mediation of that book to a general audience, and particularly so since I considered Blake, Hegel, and Nietzsche our greatest modern thinkers and visionaries of the death of God. Being persuaded that Christianity had not yet evolved a genuinely radical theology, this also became an occasion for an initial attempt to formulate a radical theology, a theology that would be systematic and biblical at once, yet nevertheless truly modern or contemporary. Of course, such an intention was too ambitious for this book, but another more realistic intention was to foster a radical theological dialogue, and in this it surely succeeded, becoming perhaps the most controversial book in our theological literature at the time, even if now, almost half a century later, both the book and that public dialogue are in deep eclipse. A comprehensive conservatism has overwhelmed the world, one that certainly dominates contemporary religion and theology, so that both radical politics and radical religion are

145

now invisible and unheard, but in the sixties they seemingly dominated discourse in the Western world, and even the Roman Catholic Church was under their impact, as witness the Second Vatican Council.

Have these radical movements vanished from our world, or do they continue in a subterranean and hidden form, perhaps now even operating in a more powerful way, and particularly so if we are facing the end of history as we have known it? It is to be remembered that Christianity began with an apocalyptic proclamation of the end of history, one that dominated the earliest Christian communities, and one that was renewed during each of the great crises or turning points of Christian history, just as it was renewed in each of our great modern political revolutions, and equally renewed in the advent of our deepest modern thinking and imaginative vision. At no point is there a more notable continuity between the modern world and an original Christianity, even if this continuity is alien to our theology, above all alien to all non-apocalyptic theology, which is to say to every theology we have known as an orthodox theology. *The Gospel of Christian Atheism* was intended to renew an apocalyptic theology, one that was born in the very advent of Christian theology in Paul, and was profoundly renewed in Blake, Hegel, and Nietzsche, who are apparently profoundly Christian at this crucial point. My second book, *Mircea Eliade and the Dialectic of the Sacred* (1963), had concluded with a theological analysis intending to draw forth the profoundly Christian ground of Nietzsche's ultimately modern vision of Eternal Recurrence, and did so in the spirit of Eliade's most treasured symbol of the *coincidentia oppositorum*, so that this book was almost inevitably followed by *The Gospel of Christian Atheism.*

If Hegel and Nietzsche are our most apocalyptic thinkers, and Blake our most apocalyptic visionary, not only are they united at this fundamental point, but this very apocalypticism is inseparable from an ultimate enactment of the death of God. Moreover, each of these primal modern figures enacted the death of God as apocalypse itself, an apocalypse that is the end of history, but that is simultaneously and precisely thereby the inauguration of a new aeon. What Blake could envision as the New Jerusalem, and Hegel could know as the advent of Absolute Spirit, and Nietzsche could envision as Eternal Recurrence, is the consequence of the end of history, an ending realized only through the death of God, which each could know as the most catastrophic ending in our history and precisely therefore as that ending able to call forth an absolute beginning.

Now if the death of God is truly fundamental in a uniquely modern apocalypticism, is that an absolute dividing line between modern apocalypticism and an original Christian apocalypticism, one revealing modern apocalypticism as an absolute desacralization or profanation of Christianity? *The Gospel of Christian Atheism* attempts to address this challenge by centering on the death of God as the deepest ground of Christianity, present even in the original proclamation of Jesus. This occurs in Jesus's unique apocalyptic enactment of the full and final advent of the Kingdom of God, for no longer is the realm of God heavenly and transcendent, as it is dawning "here" and "now," a dawning only possible as a consequence of a negation of a transcendent beyond, a negation which is a self-negation, and consequently a self-negation of Godhead itself. This is the self-negation ultimately realized in the Crucifixion, a crucifixion that Christianity has known as the one source of salvation; therein it is truly an atonement and ultimately an atonement of Godhead with itself. Just as Christian theology has never realized a genuine understanding of evil and nothingness, so it has been closed to the deep negativity of Godhead itself, or closed to the negative pole or polarity of God. Now, this is the very negativity that is profoundly realized by Blake, Hegel, and Nietzsche, and only the negation of this negativity truly effects the death of God, a negation which is apocalypse itself, and precisely therein is the apocalypse of God.

Jesus could name such an apocalypse as the Kingdom of God, and it is all too significant that Jesus is alone among ancient prophets in naming the "Kingdom of God," a naming that was at the very center of his mission, but one which soon perished in ancient Christianity. The comprehensive transformation of Christianity in the first three generations of its existence is unique in the history of religions, and nothing so deeply perished as did Jesus's apocalyptic enactment of the Kingdom of God, or, if it did not perish, it was wholly reversed, and reversed by way of a comprehensive epiphany of the absolute transcendence of God. So it is that a recovery of the original way of Jesus can occur only by way of an absolute assault upon all established or manifest Christianity, as most purely occurs in Blake and Nietzsche. But it occurs no less in Hegel, and if Hegel is the deepest center of a uniquely modern philosophical atheism, that atheism could be understood as a Christian atheism if it is understood as a reversal of a Christian transcendence of God, and a Christian transcendence that is itself a reversal of Jesus's enactment of the apocalypse of God.

An absolute immanence dominates a uniquely modern thinking and vision, one which is an inversion and reversal of a pure transcendence, hence the apocalypse of God could be understood as the final realization of the pure immanence of God, one releasing an ultimate Yes-saying, and a Yes-saying which is greeted with a pure joy. Perhaps it is joy itself that is most missing from a uniquely modern Christianity, although it is ecstatically present in both Blake and Nietzsche, but only so present as a consequence of the death of God. Hegel could know that death as the self-negation of abstract Spirit, or a wholly self-alienated Godhead, one that Blake could name as Urizen or Satan and Nietzsche could know as the deification of nothingness. Only in Hegel and Nietzsche does there finally occur a philosophical understanding of nothingness in the West, and this occurs only by way of the philosophical understanding of an absolutely self-alienated God, one which Nietzsche could know as an absolute No-saying, and one which Hegel could know as an absolute emptiness. But that is the emptiness that is created in an absolute movement of kenotic self-emptying, a movement that Hegel could understand as a repetition of the Crucifixion, and a repetition ushering in the final Age of the Spirit. So, too, Nietzsche could understand such an ultimate and final movement as the dawning of an absolute immanence, and an absolute immanence only possible as a consequence of the death of God. Only Christianity among the world religions knows the death of God, and nothing else makes Christianity so unique in the history of religions, but so likewise nothing else in modernity is more unique than its comprehensive realization of the death of God, and if nowhere else there is here a full coincidence between the depths of modernity and the depths of Christianity itself.

Must this coincidence remain closed to Christian theology? Is any genuine atheism impossible for Christian theology, and impossible if only because theology itself is inseparable from the transcendence of God? *The Gospel of Christian Atheism* claims that genuine atheism is possible only for the Christian, for only the Christian knows the actual and final death of God, a death of God alone releasing an absolute immanence, and a crucifixion releasing not an ascent into Heaven but a descent into Hell. Ancient Christianity reversed the way of the cross by knowing it as a way to a heavenly transcendence, just as it reversed the crucifixion by knowing it as resurrection, and even as a wholly otherworldly or transcendent resurrection; so too, just as the crucifixion rather than the resurrection dominates the synoptic gospels, the resurrection rather than the crucifixion dominates patristic Christianity, so much so that actual images of the crucifixion do not appear until the end of patristic Christianity. Gradually these images emerge ever more powerfully in the medieval Christian world, until they become overwhelming in the waning of the Middle Ages, then ultimately more powerful still with the birth of the modern world. This is a world with which Blake, Hegel, and Nietzsche are in profound continuity, far more so than is all manifest or ecclesiastical modern Christianity. If modernity has been wholly unable to envision resurrection, it has profoundly envisioned crucifixion, and even envisioned crucifixion as an absolute and total event.

But it cannot be a total event if it is not the death of God, and if the death of God is alien to Christian theology, it is not alien to modern thinking and vision; indeed, it is at the very center of a uniquely modern vision and thinking, and it is just for that reason that a unique modernity can be known as a Christian modernity. This is the presumption of *The Gospel of Christian Atheism*, and even if this entails a negation of ecclesiastical Christianity, this is a negation seeking a universal horizon, the universal horizon of our world. Certainly theology continues to be far distant from such a horizon, but nevertheless it is perhaps seeking it today, or is doing so wherever it is not engulfed by a new orthodoxy or new conservatism. We should understand that such orthodoxy is truly new, just as our fundamentalism is truly new, and if only such new orthodox and conservative Christianity is now seemingly alive, this could be a decisive sign of the marginalization of Christianity. On the other hand, an invisible Christianity could be very much alive today, one invisible from the viewpoint of all orthodox and ecclesiastical criteria, and nevertheless alive in our depths, though those depths be invisible to empirical observation. Is this not a situation that calls for radical theological thinking and vision, and if this can now only take place subterraneously, is it possible that genuine theological thinking can only be subterranean thinking? If so, perhaps *The Gospel of Christian Atheism* has made a contribution to our situation; if not, let it be cast into oblivion.

—AUGUST 1997

Appendix B

Altizer on Altizer: A Self-Critique

Oriental Mysticism and Biblical Eschatology (Westminster, 1961) is a tantalizing book: badly written, pretentious and irresponsible in its claims and arguments, and fundamentally lacking in historical sophistication and mastery of its sources; nevertheless it remains our only theological correlation of the original apocalyptic ground of Christianity with the higher expressions of Oriental mysticism, as here represented by Buddhism (although the original manuscript contained a chapter on Hinduism). Quite possibly this book advances a historical and theological thesis of prime importance, but it has been spoiled by premature publication and the absence of scholarly and historical mastery in its author. Despite the fact that Altizer completed a doctorate in the History of Religions at the University of Chicago, he is neither a historian nor a historian of religions. Instead he is an ersatz theologian, largely self-taught, who only employs the history of religions as a new route into a non-theological theology. This theology is grounded in the death of God, and not the death of God simply as the historical ending of Christendom, but rather the death or end or nothingness of God as the ultimate ground of Buddhism and Christianity alike. This book begins with a Nietzschean analysis of Greek thinking and literature, affirming that the distancing or dissolution of the numinous is at the center of a uniquely Greek consciousness, and while the numinous returns in Plato and Greek tragedy, this is a precarious and momentary synthesis of the numinous and the non-numinous, which soon disappears with the full advent of the Hellenistic world. Thereby a uniquely classical world disappears, as most fully effected by the very advent of Christianity, a Christianity embodying an absolute world-negation, as most purely effected in its original apocalyptic ground.

Christianity, however, is deeply grounded in the prophetic revolution of Israel, which reversed both ancient Israel and the archaic world, giving birth to a truly eschatological faith, culminating in that apocalypticism which is the womb of Christianity. This book also attempts a recovery of the original apocalyptic Jesus, one who is truly reversed by the Christian Church and the dominant Christian traditions, and who is only subsequently discovered in the most radical expressions of Christianity; but with the end of Christendom a historical recovery of the apocalyptic Jesus became possible, a recovery deeply shattering all manifest forms of Christian theology. Yet it is the apocalyptic Jesus and an apocalyptic faith that is most open to Buddhism, as each is grounded in an absolute negation of reality or the world, but these are the very negations calling forth absolute transfigurations of "Being" itself, or of the depths of actuality. Thus the book concludes with a section on faith and the Nothing, exploring a nihilism that is uniquely modern and religiously universal at once, affirming that in the higher expressions of religion, Being itself is the Other and is ultimately manifest only as the Nothing. Yet here the Nothing is finally known only through the all-consuming power of the sacred, so that the Nothing is truly a reflection or manifestation of the depths of the sacred, or of nirvana or the Kingdom of God, for just as the Buddhist comes to know samsara as nirvana, the Christian must come to know the Nothing as the hither side of Godhead itself.

Mircea Eliade and the Dialectic of the Sacred (Westminster, 1963; Greenwood Press, 1975) is another non-book, or, rather, two non-books which are only loosely and inadequately joined. The opening one is the first critical study of the scholarly work of Mircea Eliade, a study attempting to demonstrate that Eliade's dialectical understanding of the sacred is at once both genuinely modern and an authentic expression of Eastern or Orthodox Christianity. The second part is a theological rather than a scholarly analysis, advancing the claim that it is precisely the most radical expressions of the profane in the modern world that can dialectically be identified as the purest expressions of the sacred. Thus Nietzsche's vision of Eternal Recurrence is dialecti-cally identified with the uniquely Christian realization of the Kingdom of God. This dialectical identification (a Madhyamika Christianity?) is presented as the resolution of a non-dialectical contradiction in Eli-ade's understanding, one deriving from the non-dialectical ground of all established or "orthodox" Christianity, a ground which itself per-ishes with the uniquely modern realization of the death of God. One wonders how Eliade would respond to this non-book, for it attempts to unmask him as a phenomenological historian of religions and unveil him as a Christian *homo religiosus* immersed in a labyrinthine world in which God is dead. Nevertheless, Eliade could affirm that the theol-ogy of the death of God is extremely important because it is the sole religious creation of the modern Western world (*Ordeal by Labyrinth*, 151). Let it also be noted that *Mircea Eliade and the Dialectic of the Sacred* evoked what is perhaps the most brilliant and devastating satire ever written on a theological book in Walter Love's "Mercy for Miss Awdy, in a Vile Acting of the Sacred" (see appendix to Cobb, ed., *The Theology of Altizer*).

At last, in *The New Apocalypse: The Radical Christian Vision of Wil-liam Blake* (Michigan State University Press, 1967), Altizer gives us a genuine book. It is as though his long combat with Nietzsche has fi-nally given birth to him as a writer, which here occurs by way of a full conjunction of a Hegelian dialectical understanding of pure negativ-ity with the dialectical movement of the images and symbolic figures of Blake's imaginative world. Most startling of all, we discover a fully systematic theology in this book, perhaps the first genuinely radical one, and a theology purporting to be a genuine expression of a radical Christian tradition, a tradition still unknown in the world of theol-ogy. Here the Christian God, or the God of all dominant and estab-lished expressions of Christianity, is unveiled as being a Blakean Satan or a Hegelian Bad Infinite, a dark and repressive body of God who is negated and reversed by the forward and apocalyptic movement of Incarnation. At the center of this radical Christianity is the apocalyptic Christ, a total Christ, being at once the totality of a cosmic human-ity and the total embodiment of what Blake envisioned in *Milton* and *Jerusalem* as the "Self-Annihilation of God." New Testament scholars and theologians, if they would dare to enter a truly imaginative world, would be amazed to discover that it was Blake who first fully realized the eschatological or apocalyptic identity of Jesus, and that he finally succeeded in actualizing this identity as the center and ground of his greatest creations. At the end of *Jerusalem*, the absolutely sovereign and transcendent Creator and the sacrificial and self-emptying Christ dialectically and apocalyptically pass into each other, and even if such a *coincidentia oppositorum* is the deepest theological ground of Hegel's *Phenomenology of Spirit* and *Science of Logic*, such a dialectical *coincidentia* will seemingly continue to remain alien to both our ecclesiastical and theological worlds.

It is important to note that *The Gospel of Christian Atheism* (Westminster, 1966) was written after *The New Apocalypse* and is wholly dependent on that book's understanding of Blake and Hegel. Published in the same season as *Radical Theology and the Death of God* (Bobbs Merrill, 1966), a collection of essays by Altizer and William Hamilton, both books are attempts to mediate a radical theology of the death of God to the public at large. While deplored by many theologians as self-indulgence and bad taste, these books were published at a time when a theological fervor engulfed this country that is now simply inconceivable. Whether or not God was then dead, it would appear that theology soon died, or became muted as a theology directed to the fundamental question of God. So likewise there soon perished a public audience for theology, and if this was a time when an enormous gulf opened between the academic and the ecclesiastical worlds, it was also a time when the very vocation of theology threatened to disappear. Perhaps it has since wholly disappeared, as one cannot not now imagine a magazine such as *The New Yorker* devoting two consecutive issues to theology, and indeed it is odd today when a publisher of any kind releases a book of genuine theology.

In *The Descent into Hell* (Lippincott, 1970) Altizer attempted a systematic theological exploration of the radical and apocalyptic faith and enactments of both Jesus and Paul, and did so by way of a dialectical coincidence between apocalyptic Christianity and Mahayana Buddhism. Herbert Richardson identified this book as the first Buddhist Christian theology, and while this is saying too much, it certainly states the intention of the author. Once again a way is sought into the original and long forgotten apocalyptic identity of the Kingdom of God by way of a reversal of the language and movement of the Christian theological tradition, attempting to do so in the spirit of Blake's marriage of Heaven and Hell and under the deep influence of the Buddhist identification of nirvana and samsara. The deepest flaw of the book is that it is insufficiently theological; it fails fully to focus upon the self-negation or the self-emptying of God, and thus fails to realize or make manifest the acts and words of Jesus as an actualization or self-embodiment of God. Therein Altizer has also failed truly to enter the world of Buddhism, and thereby to realize a transcendence of every distinction between word and act or here and there. Above all this is a failure of imagination, and of theological imagination, a failure truly to open theological thinking to the actuality of revelation and praxis alike.

In spite of everything, Altizer intends to be a genuinely biblical theologian, being persuaded that Barth finally abandoned the Bible by choosing the final authority of the Church, so that we are now bereft of all genuinely biblical theologies. Yet Altizer's real hope and intention is to do pure theology, a theology thinking about God alone, and thinking in such a manner and mode as to make possible a theological realization of revelation. *The Self-Embodiment of God* (Harper and Row, 1977) is the purest embodiment of this intention, as it undertakes a reenactment of biblical revelation in a contemporary language, and attempts to do so by way of a meditation upon the pure actuality of speech and silence. Jacob Neusner, in a preface to a later edition of the book (University Press of America, 1985), accepted *The Self-Embodiment of God* as belonging to the sacred circle of the Torah, affirming that it is a meditative theology within that tradition. But once again Altizer attempts too much, even if the reader senses that he attempts too little. For this is an endeavor to rethink the whole movement of biblical revelation, and to do so in such a way as to make manifest its fundamental unity, a unity invisible to historical and critical understanding, yet a unity which becomes real in the very calling forth of the origin, the center, and the ending of the actuality and finality of speech itself. While this is a deeply abstract theology, and one posing formidable difficulties for its reader, this is a meditational and not an academic or scholastic theology, and if nothing else it does demonstrate the virtue of the dissolution of the theological author.

Total Presence: The Language of Jesus and the Language of Today (Seabury, 1980) is a miniature apocalyptic theology, a theology moving from the parabolic language of Jesus to a contemporary anonymity and solitude, and with the attempt to understand this movement as a consistently organic and evolutionary movement, even if its terminus brings both history and evolution to an end. Once again, this is a very abbreviated book, and one that is probably meaningless to those who do not share or are not open to its presuppositions. But it is an attempt to write a fully apocalyptic theology, and that is very rare indeed, and perhaps so rare as to be at least potentially a fundamental innovation. Yet potentiality here is not actuality, and perhaps for that very reason it may be a false potentiality unless it can become actuality in the future. Present in the background here is Bultmann's demythologizing, but whereas Bultmann was persuaded that apocalypticism is a premodern and irrecoverable mythology, Altizer is convinced that apocalypticism is the very center and ground of a uniquely modern and postmodern actuality (and is this the first theological book to discuss a postmodern theological situation?). Here the apocalyptic language of Jesus is the deepest ground of a uniquely contemporary language, and it is precisely the demythologizing of a non-apocalyptic Christianity and Christendom that is the way to that apocalypse which is being realized in our midst. Critically, *Total Presence* is most dependent upon an understanding of the Christian epic tradition as the most open and revealing expression of our apocalyptic history, but that understanding is not truly entered until Altizer's next book, *History as Apocalypse* (State University of New York Press, 1985).

History as Apocalypse is at once the first attempt to understand the Western epic tradition as an organic and evolutionary tradition beginning with Homer and ending with Joyce, and also the first attempt to understand our greatest epic poetry as the poetry of revelation, a revelation that beginning with Dante is a full embodiment of the revelation of the Bible. The central chapters here are those on Dante, Milton, Blake, and Joyce, and their epic poetry is here understood as a full conjunction of revelation and history, a history that is a revolutionary history, and a history that is at once an interior and a cosmic voyage, and a cosmic and interior voyage ever more fully and more finally embodying the finality of apocalypse itself. Religiously and politically, our epic poetry embodies our deepest heresy and subversion, an ultimate subversion that is just as fully present in Homer and Virgil as it is in Blake and Joyce, and a subversion that is fully manifest as a biblical subversion in Dante and Milton. Epic voyage is by inherent necessity a total voyage, and it either records or effects our deepest historical revolutions, but those revolutions are finally one revolution, a revolution revolving about the beginning and ending of the actuality of consciousness itself. We have long known that Homer, Dante, and Blake were the deepest epic influences on Joyce, just as we have known that Milton and later Dante were the deepest epic influences on Blake, but we have not known our epic tradition as one tradition, and even if classical epic is an all too fragile presence in *History as Apocalypse*, the Christian epic does appear here as a single epic, even if it is invisible as such in our academic and theological worlds.

Genesis and Apocalypse: A Theological Voyage Toward Authentic Christianity (Westminster John Knox, 1991) is perhaps Altizer's fullest apocalyptic theology. As such, it is in full continuity with all of his work, and fragile and tentative as that work may be, and scarred as it is by critical and scholarly shortcomings, it is a work that is the expression of a single theological voyage conducted in darkness and solitude. Of course, this voyage is an apocalyptic voyage, one now paradoxically manifest as being most openly our own and yet deeply hidden and invisible in all those languages that are now apparently real. Altizer has always been most deeply attracted by the language of scandal and offense, and here that offense may most openly occur in a total affirmation of predestination, a predestination that here is Barthian in affirming the damnation of God in Christ, and Barthian and Augustinian alike in affirming that predestination is the deepest Christian doctrine of God, but anti-Barthian and anti-Augustinian in understanding predestination as the *coincidentia oppositorum* of Christ and Satan. Augustine is the deepest theological influence here, and perhaps also throughout Altizer's work, but one that is nevertheless transcended by the profound influence of Hegel and Nietzsche, as the claim is advanced here that a modern apocalyptic voyage reverses and transcends an ancient Christian voyage, and does so by way of an apocalyptic Kingdom of God, a kingdom that was marginalized if not dissolved by the whole historical world of Christianity, except for the deepest subversions occurring in that world. This is that apocalyptic kingdom which has always been the center of the Christian epic voyage, even as it is the center of the New Testament itself, but *Genesis and Apocalypse* discovers that kingdom in the once and for all act of creation itself, a creation which is the disembodiment of an original and primordial totality, a totality most purely realized in Buddhism, and a once and for all creation which can only be consummated in apocalypse. This is the apocalypse which is celebrated and enacted throughout our Christian epic tradition, a celebration which is the celebration of a total darkness

that is finally total light, and while such light is absent in this book, a
darkness is present which is its dialectical counterpart, and if darkness
is finally light, this book may finally be theology.

A companion volume to *Genesis and Apocalypse* is *The Genesis of
God: A Theological Genealogy* (Westminster John Knox, 1993), one car-
rying forward the earlier book, but now with a total concentration on
genesis itself. Proceeding with the conviction that the orthodox doctrine of creation is perhaps our profoundest theological misunderstanding, this book attempts to reach both a purely Christological and a
purely apocalyptic understanding of genesis, understanding genesis
as being simultaneously the self-embodiment and the self-emptying
of God, and doing so not only under the impact of Spinoza, Hegel,
and Nietzsche, but also under the impact of the depths of Christian
dogmatics itself, as again the dogma of predestination is central, but
now it is understood as calling forth the ultimate depths of an absolute
nothingness that is now our deepest condition and destiny. Freedom
and nothingness are the primal categories here, a freedom that is inseparable from a fully actual nothingness, and here there is a primary
focus on the genesis both of freedom and of nothingness, a genesis that
is finally the genesis of God. Only the genesis of God could make possible the death of God, or the actual death of God; this was the problem impelling Altizer to this inquiry, and if Christianity is ultimately
unreal apart from the death of God, then so too is it unreal apart from
the genesis of God. If theology has never faced this problem before,
this is simply because it is only in our own time that theology has faced
a full and final apocalyptic crisis, a crisis demanding an understanding
of the death of God, and therefore demanding an understanding of the
genesis of God.

The Contemporary Jesus (State University of New York Press, 1997)
evoked far less public response than Altizer's other books, which is odd
given that its subject is the most popular of all theological subjects,
and this book more than any of his others is addressed to a general
audience. Altizer has been immersed in New Testament scholarship
throughout his theological career, and truly major New Testament
scholars have been among his deepest friends, but he had become ap-
palled by the diminution if not dissolution of every possible theological
ground in the dominant biblical scholarship of the past two generations, and also by the deep isolation of biblical interpretation from every possible imaginative ground, or at least of an imaginative ground

which is actually embodied in works of the imagination. Thus he became determined to write a book on Jesus that would bring together New Testament scholarship with our deepest imaginative visions of Jesus—a venture oddly enough never previously attempted—and to do so on the basis of a radical and apocalyptic theology. Again the Christian epic tradition is central here, but so likewise is the Gnostic Jesus, the Pauline Jesus, and the Buddhist Jesus, and even that nihilistic Jesus whom both Dostoevsky and Nietzsche called forth, a nihilistic Jesus who is most coincident with our contemporary world. Its final chapter attempts an unveiling of that anonymous Jesus who is the contemporary Jesus, and if this is the weakest chapter in the book, it is also the most ambitious, and therefore perhaps inevitably a failure. But is it impossible to think theologically about a Jesus who can be known either through our biblical scholarship or through our imaginative visions of Jesus? Or is it simply impossible to think theologically today?

Godhead and the Nothing (State University of New York Press, 2003) is identified by Edith Wyschogrod as a consummation of Altizer's lifework, and it is true that his earliest thinking about Godhead and the Nothing returns here, just as his continual voyaging into nihilism and an absolute nothingness now becomes even more pervasive. Yet for the first time this is a full theological entrance into the Nothing, and into a fully actual Nothing, a Nothing which can be known as absolute evil, but an absolute evil absolutely necessary to an absolute transfiguration. That apocalyptic transfiguration is the real subject of this book, thus it necessarily focuses upon evil and the Godhead, an absolute evil of the Godhead apart from which no absolute transfiguration could occur. If theology has thus far been closed to the very possibility of an absolute transfiguration, an inevitable consequence of our theology's refusal of a truly apocalyptic ground, it thereby has been closed to the possibility of an absolute evil, an absolute evil that as absolute evil is inseparable from Godhead itself. Nothing has been more theologically forbidden than a deep or ultimate thinking about evil, just as in the face of an absolute evil theology has inevitably collapsed, and if this has above all occurred in the twentieth century, no other time has so openly contended with an absolute evil.

In broaching this ultimate problem, *Godhead and the Nothing* is both a philosophical theology and a dogmatic and biblical theology, once again calling upon our most revolutionary philosophers and that Christian epic tradition which incorporates our most revolutionary imaginative expressions of the Bible. The Nothing is so pervasive here that every other perspective seemingly disappears, yet perhaps that does make possible a genuine theological entrance into our own time, a time of ultimate emptiness and darkness which only the Nothing can purely unveil. For if an absolute transfiguration is occurring even now, it could only occur through such darkness and emptiness, a truly annihilating emptiness and darkness, but an absolute annihilation is absolutely essential to an absolute transfiguration. This is above all why theology has refused the very possibility of an absolute transfiguration of the Godhead, one only partially called forth here, which is certainly a real weakness of this book and one belying its most fundamental intention.

Living the Death of God: A Theological Memoir (State University of New York Press, 2006) is not a personal memoir, and not a memoir in the common sense; it is rather an attempt to reenact my theological voyage, and as such it may well be a unique book. Its first chapter entitled "The Calling" is a difficult one if only because it is a recounting of a deep initiation into "Satan," which so largely determined my voyage. This is that Blakean Satan who is the absolutely alien God, that God whom Nietzsche knew as absolute No-saying, and that God whose Self-Annihilation is apocalypse itself. Having become persuaded that I am alone as a full apocalyptic theologian, the major task of this memoir is to recount a voyage into apocalyptic theology, one that had never previously been recorded, and perhaps never occurred before. Accordingly, this book intends to recall those fundamental movements into an apocalyptic theology, retracing my thinking and writing over a period of sixty years and attempting to recover those actual problems with which I wrestled in making these movements. This is also a tribute to those individuals who have most deeply affected me, although there is no real discussion at all of my personal life. A central problem here is an exploration of just what theology is, and here I do not mean an ecclesiastical or confessional or historical theology, but rather what I think of as fundamental theology, a theology that can only individually be enacted, and enacted through one's own thinking and one's own individual exploration.

Frankly, I think that this memoir is itself a theological statement or confession, and in retrospect I am amazed that it covers so many arenas or topics, all the way from art to predestination, and from prayer to ethics. I did attempt to speak seriously about ethics here, and to speak wholly critically about it; this entailed a return to Max Weber who so profoundly affected me, and I do think that an ethics that is indifferent to history and sociology is inevitably unreal. There can be no question that I have long been committed to doing a systematic theology, but a wholly new systematic theology, radically revising all theological categories and judgments, and most so the ultimate theological category of God or the Godhead. Simply to take this category for granted, or to presume that there is no question as to what it means, is to be nontheological, and while this is now a virtually universal condition, it makes impossible everything to which I am and have been committed. I often wonder if theology or critical theology is even being taught today, yet I am deeply impressed by the contemporary turn of philosophy to theology, just as I had been deeply affected by the rich theological thinking that has long occurred in seemingly secular circles. Many think of Hegel as a purely secular thinker, but I have long known him as the most profound of our theological thinkers, and as the creator of a totally kenotic thinking, one grounded in an absolute self-negation or self-emptying, as both apocalypse and crucifixion for the first time enter pure thinking, thereby revolutionizing thinking itself.

This is a revolution that must be incorporated into theology itself, which has been my life's task, and it would inevitably profoundly transform theology, so that my deepest regret is that my work has transformed theology far too little. Perhaps I have been alone in attempting or intending a total transformation of theology, yet I look upon this as a necessary destiny, and a necessary destiny for theology's own deepest ground. Indeed, the modern realization of the death of God is not simply an ultimate challenge to theology, it is one demanding a total transformation of theology, a transformation that actually occurs in both Hegel and Nietzsche, and one that likewise occurs in the most revolutionary expressions of the modern imagination. This is a revolution most openly embodied in Blake, who can be understood as the most revolutionary of all Christian visionaries, and simply to enter Blake theologically is to think radically theologically, which is perhaps why so few theologians have entered Blake. Certainly I was radically transformed theologically by becoming a Blakean, and I can only be grateful for that transformation, for this was my route to a new theology, and not only a new theology but a new life and world.

—July 2010

WORKS CITED

Altizer, Thomas J. J. "Apocalypticism and Modern Thinking." *Journal for Christian Theological Research* 2, no. 2 (1997): par. 1–27. http://www.apu.edu/~CTRF/jctr.html.

———. *The Contemporary Jesus*. Albany: State University of New York Press, 1997.

———. *The Descent into Hell: A Study of the Radical Reversal of the Christian Consciousness*. Philadelphia: Lippincott, 1970; reprint, New York: Seabury, 1979.

———. *Genesis and Apocalypse: A Theological Voyage Toward Authentic Christianity*. Louisville: Westminster John Knox, 1990.

———. *The Genesis of God: A Theological Genealogy*. Louisville: Westminster John Knox, 1993.

———. *Godhead and the Nothing*. Albany: State University of New York Press, 2003.

———. *The Gospel of Christian Atheism*. Philadelphia: Westminster, 1966.

———. *History as Apocalypse*. Albany: State University of New York Press, 1985.

———. *Living the Death of God: A Theological Memoir*. Albany: State University of New York Press, 2006.

———. *Mircea Eliade and the Dialectic of the Sacred*. Philadelphia: Westminster, 1963; reprint, Westport, CT: Greenwood Press, 1975.

———. "Modern Thought and Apocalypticism." In *Apocalypticism in the Modern Period and the Contemporary Age*, edited by Stephen Stein, 325–59. Vol. 3 of *Encyclopedia of Apocalypticism*. 3 vols. New York: Continuum, 1998.

———. *The New Apocalypse: The Radical Christian Vision of William Blake*. East Lansing: Michigan State University Press, 1967; reprint, Aurora, CO: Davies Group, 2000.

———. *The New Gospel of Christian Atheism*. Aurora, CO: Davies Group, 2002.

———. *Oriental Mysticism and Biblical Eschatology*. Philadelphia: Westminster, 1961.

———. "Satan as the Messiah of Nature." In *The Whirlwind in Culture: Frontiers in Theology*, edited by Donald W. Musser and Joseph L. Price, 119–34. Bloomington: Meyer-Stone Books, 1989.

———. *The Self-Embodiment of God*. New York: Harper and Row, 1977; reprint, with a preface by Jacob Neusner, Brown Classics in Judaica. Lanham, MD: University Press of America, 1985.

———. *Total Presence: The Language of Jesus and the Language of Today*. New York: Seabury, 1980.

Altizer, Thomas J. J., and William Hamilton. *Radical Theology and the Death of God*. Indianapolis: Bobbs-Merrill, 1966.

Aquinas, Thomas. *Summa Theologica*. 5 vols. Translated by the Fathers of the English Dominican Province. Westminster, MD: Christian Classics, 1948.

Augustine. *Concerning the City of God against the Pagans*. Translated by Henry Bettenson. Introduction by G. R. Evans. New York: Penguin, 2003.

———. *Confessions*. Translated by R. S. Pine-Coffin. New York: Penguin, 1961.

———. *The Trinity [De Trinitate]*. Translated by Stephen McKenna. Washington, DC: Catholic University of America Press, 1963.

Badiou, Alain. *Saint Paul: The Foundation of Universalism*. Translated by Ray Brassier. Stanford: Stanford University Press, 2003.

Barth, Karl. *Church Dogmatics*. 5 vols. Edited by G. W. Bromily and T. F. Torrance. New York: Charles Scribner's Sons, 1936–88.

Blake, William. *The Illuminated Blake: All of William Blake's Illuminated Works with a Plate-by-Plate Commentary*. Annotated by David V. Erdman. Garden City, NY: Anchor Press/Doubleday, 1974.

———. *William Blake: The Complete Illuminated Books*. Introduction by David Bindman. London and New York: Thames and Hudson in association with the William Blake Trust, 2000.

Bonhoeffer, Dietrich. *Letters and Papers from Prison*. Translated by Reginald H. Fuller. Edited by Eberhard Bethge. New York: Macmillan, 1971.

Bultmann, Rudolf. *The Theology of the New Testament*. Translated by Kendrick Grobel. Waco, TX: Baylor University Press, 2007.

Caputo, John D., and Gianni Vattimo. *After the Death of God*. Edited by Jeffrey W. Robbins. New York: Columbia University Press, 2007.

Cobb, John B., Jr. (ed.). *The Theology of Altizer: Critique and Response*. Philadelphia: Westminster Press, 1970.

Dante Alighieri. *The Divine Comedy*. 3 vols. Translated by Charles S. Singleton. Bollingen Series 80. Princeton: Princeton University Press, 1970–1975.

Depoortere, Frederiek. *The Death of God: An Investigation into the History of the Western Concept of God*. London: T and T Clark, 2007.

Dionysius the Areopagite. *On the Divine Names and the Mystical Theology*. Translated by C. E. Rolt. New York: Macmillan, 1920.

Dostoevsky, Fyodor. *The Possessed*. Translated by Constance Garnett. New York: Barnes and Noble, 2004.

Edwards, Rem B. "The Pagan Dogma of the Absolute Unchangeableness of God." *Religious Studies* 14, no. 3 (Sept. 1978): 305–13.

Eliade, Mircea. *Ordeal by Labyrinth*. Chicago: University of Chicago Press, 1982.

Eriugena, Johannes Scotus. *Periphyseon: On the Division of Nature*. Translated by Myra L. Uhlfelder. Indianapolis: Bobbs-Merrill, 1976.

Findlay, J. N. *Hegel: A Re-Examination*. New York: Macmillan, 1958.

Franke, William. "The Deaths of God in Hegel and Nietzsche." *Religion and the Arts* 11 (2007): 214–41.

Gillespie, Michael Allen. *The Theological Origins of Modernity*. Chicago: University of Chicago Press, 2008.

Goethe, Johann Wolfgang von. *Faust: A Tragedy*. Edited by Cyrus Hamlin. Translated by Walter Arndt. New York: W. W. Norton, 2001.

Harris, Matthew E. "Gianni Vattimo and Thomas J. J. Altizer on the

Incarnation and the Death of God: A Comparison." *Minerva: An Internet Journal of Philosophy* 15 (2011): 1–19. http://www.minerva.mic.ul.ie/

Hegel, G. W. F. *The Phenomenology of Spirit.* Translated by A. V. Miller with analysis of the text and foreword by J. N. Findlay. Oxford: Clarendon, 1977.

———. *Hegel's Science of Logic.* Translated by A. V. Miller. Amherst, NY: Humanity Books, 1999.

Heidegger, Martin. *Being and Time.* Translated by Joan Stambaugh. Albany: State University of New York Press, 1996.

———. *Contributions to Philosophy (From Enowning)* [*Beiträge zur Philosophie (Vom Ereignis)*]. Translated by Parvis Emad and Kenneth Maly. Bloomington: Indiana University Press, 1999.

———. *Parmenides.* Translated by André Schuwer and Richard Rojcewicz. Bloomington: Indiana University Press, 1992.

———. "Phenomenology and Theology." 1927. Translated by James G. Hart and John C. Maraldo. In *Pathmarks*, edited by William McNeill. Cambridge: Cambridge University Press, 1998.

———. *The Phenomenology of Religious Life.* Translated by Matthias Fritsch and Jennifer Anna Gosetti-Ferencei. Bloomington: Indiana University Press, 2004.

———. *Schelling's Treatise on the Essence of Human Freedom.* Translated by Joan Stambaugh. Athens: Ohio State University Press, 1985.

Hobson, Theo. "Rethinking Postmodern Theology." *Modern Believing* 47, no. 3 (July 2006): 10–20.

Joyce, James. *A Portrait of the Artist as a Young Man.* Norton Critical Edition. New York: W. W. Norton, 2001.

———. *Finnegans Wake.* New York: Penguin, 1939.

———. *Ulysses.* Introduction by Seamus Deane. New York: Penguin, 2008.

Kant, Immanuel. *Critique of Practical Reason.* Translated by Werner S. Pluhar. Introduction by Stephen Engstrom. Indianapolis: Hackett, 2002.

Kotsko, Adam. "'That They Might Have Ontology': Radical Orthodoxy and the New Debate." *Political Theology* 10, no. 1 (2009): 115–24.

———. *Žižek and Theology.* London: T and T Clark, 2008.

Leahy, D. G. *Foundation: Matter the Body Itself.* Albany: State University of New York Press, 1996.

Marion, Jean-Luc. *God without Being*. Translated by Thomas A. Carlson. Chicago: University of Chicago Press, 1995.

McCullough, Lissa. "Death of God Reprise: Altizer, Taylor, Vattimo, Caputo, Vahanian." *Journal for Cultural and Religious Theory* 9, no. 3 (Fall 2008): 97–109. http://www.jcrt.org.

———. "Theology as the Thinking of Passion Itself." In *Thinking Through the Death of God: A Critical Companion to Thomas J. J. Altizer*, ed. Lissa McCullough and Brian Schroeder. Albany: State University of New York Press, 2004.

Melville, Herman. *Moby-Dick*. Edited by Herschel Parker and Harrison Hayford. Norton Critical Edition. New York: W. W. Norton, 2002.

Milton, John. *Christian Doctrine*. Edited by Maurice Kelly. Translated by John Carey. Vol. 6 of *The Complete Prose Works of John Milton*. New Haven: Yale University Press, 1973.

———. *Paradise Lost*. Edited by John Leonard. New York: Penguin, 2003.

Nietzsche, Friedrich. *The Gay Science*. Translated by Walter Kaufmann. New York: Random House, 1974.

———. *On the Genealogy of Morals*. Edited by Walter Kaufman. Translated by R. J. Hollingdale and Walter Kaufmann. New York: Vintage, 1967.

———. *Thus Spoke Zarathustra: A Book for All and None*. Translated by Walter Kaufmann. New York: Penguin, 1954.

———. *Twilight of the Idols and The Anti-Christ*. Translated by R. J. Hollingdale. Introduction by Michael Tanner. New York: Penguin, 1990.

Oventile, Robert S. "Let God Die." *Stirrings Still: International Journal of Existential Literature* 1, no. 1 (Fall 2004): 74–82.

Robbins, Jeffrey W. *In Search of a Non-Dogmatic Theology*. Aurora, CO: Davies Group, 2004.

Rorty, Richard, and Gianni Vattimo. *The Future of Religion*. Edited by Santiago Zabala. New York: Columbia University Press, 2005.

Schelling, F. W. J. *Philosophical Investigations into the Essence of Human Freedom*. Translated by Jeff Love and Johannes Schmidt. Albany: State University of New York Press, 2006.

Schweitzer, Albert. *The Mysticism of Paul the Apostle*. Translated by William Montgomery. Baltimore: Johns Hopkins University Press, 1998.

Tillich, Paul. *Systematic Theology*. 3 vols. Chicago: University of Chicago Press, 1951–1963.

Tolstoy, Leo. *Anna Karenina*. Translated by Richard Pevear and Larissa Volokhonsky. New York: Viking, 2001.

Vattimo, Gianni. *After Christianity*. Translated by Luca D'Isanto. New York: Columbia University Press, 2002.

———. *Belief*. Translated by Luca D'Isanto and David Webb. Stanford: Stanford University Press, 1999.

Weber, Max. *The Protestant Ethic and the Spirit of Capitalism*. Translated by Talcott Parsons. Edited by Richard Swedberg. Norton Critical Edition. New York: W. W. Norton, 2008.

Weisheipl, James A. *Friar Thomas D'Aquino: His Life, Thought, and Works*. Washington, DC: Catholic University of America Press, 1983.

Wiesel, Elie. *Night*. New York: Avon, 1969.

Žižek, Slavoj. "Dialectical Clarity versus the Misty Conceit of Paradox." In *The Monstrosity of Christ: Paradox or Dialectic*, ed. Creston Davis, 234–306. Cambridge: MIT, 2009.

———. *In Defense of Lost Causes*. London: Verso, 2008.

Index